Zinnie Harris

PLAYS ONE

Zinnie Harris's plays include the multi-award-winning *Further than the Furthest Thing* (National Theatre/Tron Theatre; winner of the 1999 Peggy Ramsay Award, 2001 John Whiting Award, Edinburgh Fringe First Award), *How to Hold Your Breath* (Royal Court Theatre; joint winner of the Berwin Lee Award), *The Wheel* (National Theatre of Scotland; joint winner of the 2011 Amnesty International Freedom of Expression Award, Fringe First Award), *Nightingale and Chase* (Royal Court Theatre), *Midwinter, Solstice* (both RSC), *Fall* (Traverse Theatre/RSC), *By Many Wounds* (Hampstead Theatre) the trilogy *This Restless House*, based on Aeschylus' *Oresteia* (Citizens Theatre/National Theatre of Scotland; Best New Play, Critics Award for Theatre in Scotland) and *Meet Me at Dawn* (Traverse Theatre). Also she adapted Ibsen's *A Doll's House* for the Donmar Warehouse, Strindberg's *Miss Julie* for the National Theatre of Scotland, *(Fall of) The Master Builder* for Leeds Playhouse and *The Duchess (of Malfi)* for the Royal Lyceum Theatre, Edinburgh. She received an Arts Foundation Fellowship for playwriting, and was Writer in Residence at the RSC, 2000–2001. She is Professor of Playwriting and Screenwriting at the University of St Andrews, and was the Associate Director at the Traverse Theatre 2015–2018.

T0322884

also by Zinnie Harris from Faber

ZINNIE HARRIS

Plays One

Further than the Furthest Thing

Midwinter

How to Hold Your Breath

Meet Me at Dawn

with an introduction by
Dominic Hill

FABER & FABER

First published in 2019
by Faber and Faber Limited
The Bindery, 51 Hatton Garden
London EC1N 8HN

Typeset by Country Setting, Kingsdown, Kent CT14 8ES
Printed in England by CPI Group (UK) Ltd, Croydon CR0 4YY

A CIP record for this book is available from the British Library

ISBN 978–0–571–35672–0

Printed and bound in the UK on FSC® certified paper in line with our continuing
commitment to ethical business practices, sustainability and the environment.
For further information see faber.co.uk/environmental-policy

2 4 6 8 10 9 7 5

Contents

Introduction

A dead horse. A woman.

The woman drags the horse on to the centre of the stage,

She takes out a large sharpened stone and starts to hack at the horse's flesh.

These words, the opening stage directions to *Midwinter*, were my first encounter with Zinnie Harris's plays and, immediately, I was hooked. Stories of survival and brutality, strong characters (usually women) in desperate situations who are forced to confront a problem of huge personal importance – this is the substance of Harris's work.

Since that first powerful taste, I've directed a number of her plays and, if I stray from the four contained within this volume, it is because I relish the whole body of her work and see it in its entirety. She knows how to engage an audience through startling imagery, plot and stagecraft, seamlessly embedding physical dramatic action to create often shocking or surprising events. Whether it is the smashing of the Pinnawin 'eggs' in the first scene of *Further than the Furthest Thing* or the blinding of Grenville in *Midwinter*, she keeps us on the edge of our seats.

Taking place in their own timeless worlds and exploring eternal themes, the plays exhibit, at their heart, an overwhelming belief in humanity, albeit a humanity pitted against destructive and inescapable laws and events. There is the fast-moving modernisation championed by Mr Hansen in the intriguingly entitled *Further than the Furthest Thing*, the returning war of *Midwinter*, the demands of justice in *Fall* and the cry for revenge in Harris's superb rewriting of Aeschylus' *Oresteia*, *This Restless House*. How is it possible to deal with these epic demands and problems, she asks, when they are out to crush and destroy?

The first play in this collection, the hugely successful *Further than the Furthest Thing*, is based loosely on family history, the opening act set on an island similar to Tristan de Cunha, where Harris's mother spent the first few years of her life. This British Overseas Territory is the remotest inhabited island on the planet, located almost equidistantly between South Africa and Argentina. When a volcano erupts, a cautious, isolated community who are familiar only with a way of life that has not changed since the Napoleonic wars, with its idiosyncratic language and shared, dark history, is evacuated to England. Their homemade island dwellings are swapped for the damp social housing of Southampton and their subsistence economy is replaced by industrial capitalism. The play asks what value these people have to us in our modern capitalist world and questions how important is the preservation of their way of life in the face of economic and social change. It is a recurring theme. The leading character is Mill: birdlike and idiosyncratic with an iron determination. She was played originally by Paola Dionisotti, in an unforgettable, hilarious performance, which savoured the play's rich language:

> Is no crawfish and Pinnawin H'eggs
> Is the Queen now
> And puddings
> And is no more watching weeks and weeks for a boat
> and looking and looking
> Is going up in a lift
> And wearing a mac
> A mac-in-tosh
> Is no more collecting sea shells
> Is cinema on Sundays
> And umbrellas

In *Midwinter*, Maud shares Mill's determination to survive and is willing to go to greater extremes. Commissioned by the Royal Shakespeare Company, it is the first in a trilogy of war plays. *Solstice* followed and then the mighty, and underrated, *Fall*. *Solstice* takes place before the start of an unnamed war, *Midwinter* in its midst, and *Fall* in its aftermath, exploring a society trying to pick up the pieces and create a democracy. The work offers an unflinching depiction of violence and brutality, unafraid to lay bare humanity's capacity for ugliness, animalistic tendencies (Harris has a degree in biology) and selfishness. But although *Midwinter* takes place against the clamour of war, there is also a quietness, a beauty and domesticity, as so often in Harris's writing. At its close, we are asked: how do we survive in a world that is at war with itself – a world so brutal that children are trained as soldiers and return home with blinding parasites in their eyes? One answer, and it's a tempting one, is that we turn our back and look towards our homes, our children, our bare gardens, where we might try to grow a few herbs:

> **Maud** What we are is what we are here. That's all. Nothing more. Three souls and a house.
> And a sky and a sun.
> A garden.

Because, for all the darkness in Harris's work, there is always a shred of hope, a ray of light.

The trilogy questions how we deal with living comfortably in the West while these atrocities take place elsewhere. *How to Hold Your Breath* takes this idea further – and closer to home – pitting the central character Dana (electrifyingly portrayed by Maxine Peake in the original production) against the collapse of European society. In a series of startlingly prescient and terrifying scenes, Dana and her sister Jasmine travel from Berlin to Alexandria, while first the banking system and then society itself disintegrate around them. How quickly the sisters are homeless and forced into prostitution, ending up us destitute migrants in a boat in the Mediterranean, seems frighteningly plausible. Harris paints a recognisably privileged world and demonstrates the fragility of that existence. Here, academia becomes meaningless in the face of practical survival; the self-help books suggested by the Librarian are useless.

Harris is not frightened of entertaining the magical and the supernatural, the possibility of gods and other powers. In *Further than the Furthest Thing*, Bill clings on to a sense of another power within the island; in *Meet Me at Dawn* the homeless woman who sleeps in the garage seems to have supernatural sway; the ghost of Iphigenia haunts *This Restless House*; and, in her latest play, *The Duchess (of Malfi)*, Harris's theatrical sensibility blends beautifully with Webster's to give us a ghost-infested reality. So it is perhaps not surprising that *How to Hold Your Breath* opens with Dana sleeping with the Devil himself, an act that seems to precipitate the collapse of society. It ends with a chilling scene in which the Devil and the Librarian, an enigmatic and morally ambiguous character, stand over the body of Dana and decide whether or not to let her live. The Librarian says:

> But her eyes are open now, she can't shut them again. What she has seen – she thought that men and women were basically good, human nature in essence benign. Then she saw it all wash away, one crisis and the jungle came at her, she heard the hyenas howling, saw hell etched on other people's faces. Let's face it she saw the dark swamp at the bottom of the human soul and once you have seen that –

To me this encapsulates the work of Zinnie Harris. The characters in her plays are forced to encounter 'the dark swamp' and, having seen it, must learn how, or even if, they are able to carry on. And we, the audience, are asked to engage with these same questions.

Meet Me at Dawn is quieter and more intimate than the previous plays. But no less devastating. It asks, 'What would you do if you were given one more day with your deceased loved one?' Here Harris was influenced by the Orpheus and Eurydice myth – all her works have the universality and mythic possibilities of ancient Greek legend – but she takes the idea of Orpheus's desperation to see his beloved and makes it her own. The play opens almost as a lyrical puzzle for the audience: where are we, what's happening, what does that signify? And then we witness a beautiful, shattering evocation of love and how it might feel if that love were snatched away. It is perhaps the most intensely personal of Harris's plays, nevertheless positioned within a timeless landscape, its superb stagecraft keeping a potentially static situation constantly alive and surprising. Again, it demonstrates, ultimately, an unceasing belief in the strength and goodness of the human spirit. Lighting a fire, the final image, echoes the end of her much earlier play, *Fall*, in which a pregnant woman and a stranger flee a war-torn city. It reminds us of the humanity and enduring hope at the heart of Harris' work. It is the work of one of our greatest living dramatists.

Liddel I am not leaving you. Not now.
It's you, me, and the baby now.

Kiki And this world of nothing.
How long is it until the sun has fully gone down do you think?

Liddel A few minutes.
We still have a few matches left, remember.

Kiki Yes, we still have a few matches.

Dominic Hill
June 2019

Artistic Director at the Citizens Theatre, Glasgow

FURTHER THAN
THE FURTHEST THING

Author's Note

Further than the Furthest Thing is set on a remote island in the middle of the Atlantic, based loosely on the real island of Tristan da Cunha. The island is as far from Cape Town in one direction as South America in the other, and its only contact with the outside world is a ship that visits approximately every six months. Although the year is 1961, the extreme isolation has meant that the islanders are an odd hybrid of cultures and periods, part Napoleonic, part Victorian and part modern in dress, accent and attitude. The men wear trousers, jackets and flat caps, the women patterned dresses and headscarves. Both sexes wear very thick white socks knitted with yarn made from flax. The island community is around 170 people, made from seven families descended from the original seven shipwrecked sailors who started the colony centuries before. There is neither electricity nor trees on the island, so the houses are entirely lit by lamplight and made of stone and planks salvaged from shipwrecks.

Further than the Furthest Thing owes much to the Tristan islanders and their story, the story of their beautiful island and isolated lifestyle that was dramatically interrupted when the volcano erupted and the entire community was evacuated to Southampton. However, the story is not solely their own and departs from accurate documentation almost immediately. In many ways I stole the real Tristan da Cunha to feed my imagination, and emerged gorged, to write into existence a host of characters and events that never happened. Anyone who is sufficiently interested in discovering the true story of their evacuation and history should take the time to read some of the many books that have been written about it – they will find the real version is richer still.

My own connection with Tristan da Cunha started when my grandfather was posted there as an Anglican priest soon after the Second World War. He took with him my grandmother, then a young woman, and my mother and aunt as children. Although they only spent a few years there, it went into family mythology, and we all grew up on tales of this magical place. We spent many evenings poring over hazy photographs of men with strangely serious faces, we were told about long boats, penguin eggs, black volcanic sand and places that were called things like 'The Patches' or 'The Ugly Road'. My mother still on occasion eats potato raw, claiming she prefers it, and she and my aunt can still remember being told about the 'H'outside Warld' as someone might tell a fairytale. It is to this Tristan, the Tristan of childhood memories, with fuzzy edges and missing bits, that this play is dedicated. And also, of course, to my Mum.

Zinnie Harris
August 2000

Further than the Furthest Thing, a co-production between the Tron Theatre Company, Glasgow, and the National Theatre, London, was first performed at the Traverse Theatre, Edinburgh, on 6 August 2000, and subsequently at the Tron Theatre, Glasgow, on 6 September 2000, and on the Cottesloe stage of the National Theatre on 5 October 2000. The cast, in order of speaking, was as follows:

Mill Lavarello Paola Dionisotti
Francis Swain Gary McInnes
Bill Lavarello Kevin McMonagle
Mr Hansen Darrell D'Silva
Rebecca Rodgers Arlene Cockburn

Director Irina Brown
Designer Niki Turner
Lighting Designer Neil Austin
Music Gary Yershon
Sound Designer Duncan Chave
Movement Director Jackie Matthews
Company Voice Work Patsy Rodenburg

Cimbalom played by Greg Knowles

Characters

Mill
Bill
Francis
Rebecca
Mr Hansen

Act One

SCENE ONE

Bill is standing by the edge of the mountain lake.

He takes off his clothes and steps into the water. It is very cold.

He reaches down to wet his arms and face.

He puts his shoulders under the surface and swims.

A terrible rumbling begins under the water.

The noise becomes more and more deafening.

Bill panics, trying to swim back to the shore. He nearly drowns but manages to haul himself on to the bank.

After he has caught his breath he stands up and turns around to look at the water . . .

There is silence.

SCENE TWO

Mill and Francis, inside Mill's house. They are in the main room which is very bare apart from the walls which are plastered with dated (1950s) magazine cuttings.

Francis has just walked in.

Mill
  Been waiting. Since sun is first come up.
  I's seeing your ship from the first it was.

9

I's holding my breath for the rocks. Shutting my eyes
for the corner.
Counting my heart's beating as in it came.

Francis

Mill . . .

Mill

Don't come near, just as yet.
Let me be seeing you first
The other way
So these is what they is wearing, H'outside there
then?
Your uncle's been a missing you.
He's an old man. You shouldn't be as going off from
an old man.

Francis

Only been gone . . .

Mill

Months
Months and months
I is counted Francis
Is half the year and half again

Francis

There was no boat

Mill

Don't come near me, I's still looking at you.
Had two weddings
Two weddings
And lots of birthdays
Harry Repetto is died.
Missed that. See – missed Harry Repetto is died.
Is dead second Sunday after you left.
Where's your bag?

Francis
On the shore

Mill
Said don't touch me. I's still making sure it is you.

Pause.

A Hagan is married a Glass and a Hagan is married
a Green
And you is missed both.
And Harry Repetto . . .

Francis
Is that all is married?

Mill
Is two weddings Francis

Francis
She wasn't on the shore

Mill
She'll be along

*Mill looks around, awkward and wanting to find
something to show him.*

She indicates the walls.

Boat you left on is bringing us whole load of pictures.
Is all new Francis

Francis looks around at the walls.

Francis
I like it

Mill
Do you?
Is the Queen.
There.
As is sitting on her throne in H'England.

And that's some mountains somewhere
Is never seeing those mountains is you?

Francis

No

Mill

Is needing to look at them before saying 'No', Francis.

Francis

I didn't see those mountains

Mill

Anyway, is a mountain here.
No need to go away and see a mountain, we've got
    one here.
Just some pictures, Francis. I is taking them down
    soon.

Pause.

You wanting an H'egg?
Got one, is for you.
Could boil it up for you.

Francis

No thanks

Mill

Wouldn't be taking a second

Francis

I'm not hungry

Mill

You always is hungry.

Francis

No Mill

Pause.

Mill

A cup of tea?

Francis

I'm fine as I am

Mill

The Queen is taking tea in the afternoon. And Prince
What's His Name.

Pause.

Where was you saying your bag was?

Francis

On the shore

Pause.

Mill

Can't be thinking what else there is. Must as be
something else is happened. Your uncle be pleased
to see you anyway.
I suppose you is seen the church?
Roof is pulled down to be making Harry Repetto's
coffin. So that is that.
Church isn't being the same when the rain is running
down your neck.

Francis

Mill?

Mill

What?

Francis

Am I allowed to come and kiss you yet?

Mill isn't sure as she goes towards him.

Then she almost bursts into tears as she hugs him.

Bill enters, looking confused.

Bill

Something in the water.

Mill mops her tears.

Something terrible under the water, underneath where
it is dark. Mill I's heard something . . .

Mill

Bill?

She nods towards Francis.

Bill stops and sees Francis for the first time.

Francis

Hallo Uncle Bill.

Pause.

Bill

Francis.

*Bill holds out both hands. Francis takes them, but they
are awkward with each other.*

Bill

Is something in the water lad

Mill

I was telling him that we's been missing him.

Bill

Heard it when I put my head under, like a great
juddering . . .

Mill

He is just stepped off the boat

Bill

No time to waste Mill, might have gone by the time
we's getting back there.

Mill

We's just going to get his bag

Bill stops.

Bill
His bag?

Mill
From the shore.

Bill
Can wait, can't it lad?

Francis
Maybe it was the wind

Bill
Was bigger than the wind, and under. Was under like a wave of thunder.

Mill
You never mind him Francis, is more like a fool every day

Bill
And when I came out, it was as like these hands were a pulling at me

Mill
Bill, in heaven's name. The lad is just walked off the boat after is gone for months and months

Bill
Francis look at me. My legs is shaking

Mill
You is carrying on like this and I is making you shake.

Francis
It's alright Aunty Milly

Bill
I was not even having time to let my clothes dry. I was

that scared, that I's just running down the hill.
Look at that.

Bill sits down and takes his shoes off.

Mill

He's as pleased to see you as I am. Underneath.

Bill

I's telling you there is something in the water.
Is something in the water

*Bill goes over to the table where there is a jug of water.
He holds it up to the light.*

Mill

He is been so excited about you coming

*Bill tastes the water. Then he puts his ear right up close
to the jug and listens.*

Mill wrings her hands.

Is having one of his off days.

Francis shrugs.

Francis

It doesn't matter.

Pause. They watch Bill, who is absorbed.

I've got a surprise for you

Mill

For me?

Francis

For all of you.
With my bag.
Down on the shore

Mill

Oh?

Francis
  I'll go and get it.

Francis starts to leave, as he goes he steps back in.

  Oh and Aunty . . .

Mill
  Yes?

Francis
  I's glad to be back.

Bill is still muttering to the water and pouring it over his fingers.

Mill waits until Francis has gone, then turns on Bill.

Mill
  You

Bill
  What?

Mill
  Going on like that

Bill
  I's telling you there is . . .

Mill
  I is not wanting to hear it Bill. Is months and months away and is only just walked in the door, and you is going on about . . .

Bill
  I'm scared Mill.

Mill
  Is rubbish

Bill
  Is no good. Whatever it is. Is no good.

Pause.

Mill

You is always the same.

Francis and you. Ever since Francis is a boy you and he won't be looking at each other and saying, 'Is good to see you'. 'Is good to see you' . . . And do not be thinking that you is going anywhere, you is going nowhere until we is finished all sitting down and eating. Like a family.

Bill

But Mill . . .

Mill

You is staying right here

Bill stops what he is doing.

You can be going in the morning
Is been away for months and months . . .
Is good to see him, isn't it Bill?

Bill

Of course is good to see him

Pause.

Mill

Just because is not your family

Bill

No

Mill

When you is looking at him you's seeing Swain

Bill

I's seeing Francis

Mill

I's seeing my sister

Pause.

Bill

Of course is good to see him Mill

Mill

He's been away

Bill

I know

Mill

I's wanting it to be special

Mill takes the jug back and puts it on the table. Bill stands up.

I've got H'eggs

Bill says nothing.

Mill shows him three in a basket.

Mill

Pinnawin H'eggs

Bill

Milly?

Mill shrugs.

Mill

Tonight is as going to be special

Bill

Pinnawin?

Mill

They's had plenty

Bill

Who?

Mill

I is found them

Bill

You's shouldn't have gone touching them

Mill

They's wasn't in a nest

Bill

You's should have left them be

Mill

They's just on the path, left

Bill

They's have come back for them

Mill

Tonight is the night Francis is come home

Bill

It's bad luck to take a pinnawin one

Mill

Tch

Bill

We isn't needing any more bad luck
You should have been leaving them

Mill

Tastes nice though
Pinnawin H'eggs
Haven't had a Pinnawin H'egg since
Long long time
Since the day your pa is dead

Bill

We was having one then?

Mill

We all was.

Pause.

Shall I be taking them back now?

Bill

I don't know

Mill
Could easy

Bill gets out three plates.

Bill
Well now they're here.

Mill
You is a good man Bill Lavarello.

Pause.

They both start laying the table.

Francis was saying that he is got a surprise for us.

Bill
Oh

Mill
Surprise is as come from the H'outside World

Bill
Oh

Mill
Never been having a surprise before
Could be some more pictures.
Or some sugar
You remember when the last boat came and was
    bringing us all some sugar?
Maybe is sugar?

Bill
Maybe is

Bill carries out the eggs and puts them in a pan.

Mill
You need to be putting water in the kettle Bill

Bill reluctantly goes to fill the pan with water.

Wait
They's beautiful

Bill

Was we really eating them the day my pa was dying?

Mill

Yes

Bill

Fancy you is remembering that

Mill

Let me be holding one for a second

Bill offers her the pan. She takes one out.

Is still warm

She takes the other one out, so she is holding two, one in each hand.

She tries to take the third one out, but as she does so it rolls off her hand.

It smashes on the floor.

They stare at it.

Pause.

Bill

Now that is bad luck

Mill

Don't Bill

Bill

I'll get a cloth

Mill

Maybe we's could . . .

She attempts to scoop it up with the shells, still holding the other two eggs.

Bill
No

Mill
Is waste

Bill
Doesn't matter

Mill
Waste of a life, I mean
A little pinnawin is gone smash on our floor.

Bill
Mill?

Mill
I shouldn't have took it

Bill
I'll clear it up

Mill
Shouldn't have gone taking them should I?
I was so wanting it to be special

Bill
I know

Bill lifts the remaining two out of her hands and puts them in the pot.

Is two left Mill.
You and Francis have them

Mill
No no.
Not me

Bill
We can share them, they's big ones.
Plenty for us all Mill

Mill

I shouldn't have gone taken them anyway

Bill bends down and clears up the mess.

I is not seeing how they is bad luck.

They is only an H'egg. How can an H'egg be as bad luck.

How can something is new life be as bad luck?

Bill

I don't know

Maybe is because it is new life and we's eating it as is bad luck.

Mill

No one says that about crawfish. Or potatoes. They is life isn't they?

Bill

Suppose

Mill

Anyway we's already had all our bad luck as is due us.

Bill stiffens as he puts the broken egg in the bin.

Mill goes back over to the pot.

She takes one out again.

Was just holding it to say is still warm.

Still warm Bill.

She takes the other one out.

Bill

Careful Mill

Mill

I is careful

You is wanting a hold?

Bill

No

Mill

Hold it Bill. Feel as is still warm.

Bill puts down the dustpan and brush and holds one.

And th'other.

Mill hands over the other, but Bill doesn't have it properly. He drops it.

They stare at the second broken egg.

Mill starts to wail.

Bill

Doesn't matter
Doesn't matter Mill. Is still one left, isn't there?
That one we is kept for Francis.
Francis is needing them, you and me isn't.

Bill is still holding the third egg

Mill

I shouldn't have gone taking them

Bill

Doesn't matter

Bill puts the third egg back in the pan.

Mill

You is right, the adult birds would have come back
    for them, course they would.
Imagine if that is me. If I's that bird and I's coming
    back and seeing them gone . . .

Bill says nothing, he just watches her.

Only it could never be me, could it?

Bill

Francis will be back soon.
He can have the last H'egg.

Bill puts the pan on to the stove.

Mill

He was saying he's got us a surprise

He sits her down.

He gets out three mugs and puts them on the table as he talks.

Bill

I was seeing you waiting today
I was seeing you from the mountain
I was seeing you standing on the shore
A tiny speck
But I was knowing it was you

Mill begins to lose her daze.

I was telling from the way you was standing that you
was holding your breath.

Mill

I couldn't watch

Bill

I could tell.
You was shutting your eyes

Mill

I was not wanting to see

Bill

I could tell

Mill

Why didn't you come down?

Bill

I don't know

Mill

You could have been waiting with me

Bill

I was wanting to but . . .

I needed to swim.
The water was . . . I was wanting to.
I was needing to swim.

Mill
Oh.

Bill
Only then I was not able

Mill hears the sound of footsteps on the path.

She goes to the window.

Mill
Is coming back. Bill – is coming back. Is that boiling?

Bill
Boiling

Mill
Maybe it'll be sugar as brought us.
Big sack of sugar.

Francis comes back in. He is carrying a brown leather briefcase, once smart, now worn.

Mill is surprised by how small it is.

That your bag?

Francis
I don't need much

Mill
Oh

Mill has a good look at the bag.

Isn't yours is it?

Francis
I was given it.

Bill
　　We's doing your H'egg

Francis
　　Thanks

Bill
　　Come and be sitting

Francis
　　It's strange to be back
　　Good and strange
　　It's like nothing has happened

Mill
　　Two weddings is happened
　　And Harry Repetto

Francis
　　Nothing is really happened.

Bill puts one egg-cup on the table.

　　Aren't you having one?

Bill
　　We has smashed them, as a mistake

Francis
　　Oh

Bill
　　One left, is for you

Francis
　　Thanks
　　I brought the surprise

Mill
　　Oh?

Francis
　　Well, it's a sort of surprise

Mill

Oh .

Francis

Not a gift, just a . . .

Bill and Mill look surprised.

Someone I want you to meet. A friend of mine.
I brought him home with me

Francis goes to the door.

Come on.
Aunty Mill and Uncle Bill, this is Mr Hansen

Mr Hansen walks in.

Nobody says anything.

Take a seat

Mr Hansen brushes the chair then sits down.

Mr Hansen is from Cape Town

Pause. Mill and Bill don't like the look of him.

Mill

We only has one H'egg

Francis

Mr Hansen can have it

Mill

You must be having the H'egg Francis

Francis

Mr Hansen owns a factory in Cape Town.

Pause.

The largest factory in the whole of Cape Town

Pause.

When you arrive at the harbour it is the only thing
you can see, like a great giant staring up at you.

Then as you get closer you can see people and
    machinery and windows and smoke, lots of smoke
And he employs thousands of workers. Don't you?
Thousands of people. And wherever you go in Cape
Town, everyone has heard of Mr Hansen.
And ask him what the factory makes. Go on ask him
    what it makes.

Bill
What does it make?

Mr Hansen
Jars

Francis
Not just jars

Mr Hansen
And cans.

Francis
And boxes. All kind of boxes.

Mr Hansen
Containers generally

Bill
You must be needing a lot of containers in Cape Town.

Mr Hansen
We are.

Francis
Not just Cape Town, Mr Hansen has factories all
    over the world.

Mr Hansen
Small factories

Mill
You is never making anything to be putting in the jars?

Mr Hansen
No

Mill
Oh
Sounds like is exciting
Never been hearing of a factory that made just jars.

Bill
I's afraid you's going to find us rather dull Mr Hansen.
There is no factories on the island. Just the mountain
and the patches.

Mr Hansen
Francis told me a little of what it would be like.

Bill
How long is you staying?

Mr Hansen
Two days.

Francis
Until the ship leaves again

Bill
Well you is welcome, isn't he Milly?

Francis
Mr Hansen is staying on the ship Uncle Bill.

Bill
Oh.

Mill
Are you going to eat that H'egg?

Pause.

Are you going to eat that H'egg?

Mr Hansen
Thank you, yes.

Mill
We did have more but they as got smashed. If we had
been knowing we was having guests this night, that

is to say not just Francis, we would have got more,
is as so Bill?
We is eating a lot of these kind of H'eggs up here.

Pause.

You is wanting a cup of tea to go with that Mr Hansen?

Mr Hansen
Thank you no.

Mill
I know you's maybe is thinking we is simple living as
like this, but we's from the island and we is used
to it. We is not needing any fancy stuff. We's got
potatoes hasn't we? And carrots and crawfish, and
four cows up by the school and even if as our
church hasn't got a roof just at the minute when
you is singing the way we is singing on the island,
who is needing a roof?

Pause.

Mr Hansen nods in agreement.

Mr Hansen
Indeed.

Mill
So don't you go wiping our chairs before you is sitting
down.

Pause.

Mr Hansen stands up.

Mr Hansen
I should be going.
Mr Swain. Mrs Swain

Mill
Lavarello
Francis is Swain. We is Lavarello

Mr Hansen

Apologies. Mrs Lavarello.
I should be getting back

Mill

You isn't finished your H'egg as yet

Mr Hansen isn't sure.

We doesn't go wasting things here either

Mr Hansen sits down.

Mr Hansen

It's a very beautiful island Mr Lavarello

Bill

We's knowing it.
None other is so beautiful I shouldn't think, whole of
the ocean.

Mill

Well finish it then

Bill

Leave him be Mill

Mill

I's only saying he's to finish it before it gets cold

Mr Hansen

Let me show you something

He eats the egg quickly by putting several mouthfuls in his mouth.

Mr Hansen holds up his empty eggshell to show them.

He swallows.

Mr Hansen

See, nothing there.

He places the egg on the table and smashes it into fragments with his fist.

He then takes out a handkerchief and puts the egg fragments into it.

He blows on the bundle.

Then he opens up the handkerchief again and produces a glass jar.

Mill gasps, Bill is more suspicious.

Mill
Where is the H'egg shell has gone?

Mr Hansen
Vanished

He shows her the handkerchief which is empty.

He also shows her his two hands and shows that there is nothing up his shirt sleeves.

Mill takes the jar and looks it over.

Mill
Is real
Look Bill, is real

Mr Hansen stands up again.

Mr Hansen
I really should be going now. You've been most kind.

Francis
There is no need

Mr Hansen
They lock up the ship at night

Mill
Let me see that cloth.

Mr Hansen hands her the cloth. Mill inspects it both sides.

Do it again

Bill
Mill be leaving him be, is having to get back now

Mill

You is not minding my asking are you Mr Hansen?

Mr Hansen

It's nothing really

Mill

They'll not be locking the ship without you.

Mr Hansen looks at Francis.

Francis will be walking you back when we is done

Mr Hansen picks up the jar and wraps it in the handkerchief.

He bangs the whole lot down on the table.

He blows on it.

Then he opens the handkerchief to reveal a new, differently coloured intact egg again. He gives her the egg.

Mill

As it is
Would you be seeing that Bill if I wasn't here showing
    it to you? Look at it.
Would you now?

She shows it to Bill.

Is a new H'egg

She passes it around.

They look with some wonder at Mr Hansen.

A new H'egg. Feel like is just been laid.
How is that happening?
Where is the jar gone?

Mr Hansen

Same place as the egg went

Mill once again looks all through the handkerchief.

Mill

Bet you couldn't be doing it a third time

Bill

Mill, Mr Hansen is our guest

Mill

Third time, is the thing. Yous may been doing it once, twice, but could you be doing it for a third time?
Once more
Once more and I won't be going asking you favours again. After all you's gone and made our H'eggshell disappear and then given us a jar and then that is gone again now

Mr Hansen

You have a new egg

Mill

I was liking more the jar

Mr Hansen

You can't bargain with magic

She hands the handkerchief back.

Mill

Once more

Mr Hansen

Then I must go
Agreed?

She nods.

Give me the egg

Mill doesn't want to part with it.

The egg or I can't do it

She gives him the egg.

I'll tell you a story first
It's a story about a jar

The first time I saw a jar I was four years old
Standing in front of a sweet shop
Most children would have been looking at the sweets
But I was looking at the jars
A brown glass jar with a lid
And behind it another
Rows and rows of them, little ones, big ones
Jars with screw lids, cork lids, without any lids at all
And from that moment I knew
I was hooked
The rest of my life I was going to spend buying them,
    selling them,
Making them
It might sound simple to you Mrs Lavarello
But jars are my life

Once again he puts the egg in the handkerchief, bangs it on the table, then blows on it.

He pauses, holding the effect.

They are all intent on what it will have become, although when Mr Hansen catches Bill's eye, Bill pretends not to be interested.

He opens the handkerchief to reveal a handful of coins.

He puts the coins into Mill's hands. Mill is enchanted.

Bill jumps up.

Bill
    Put them away

Mill
    Sit down Bill

Bill
    We aren't be wanting them. Give them back Mill,
    here be giving them back to Mr Hansen

Mill
He gave them to me

Bill tries to snatch them.

Bill
Mill

Mill
No

Bill
They belongs to Mr Hansen

Mill
I's the one holding them

Bill
They is coming from inside of his handkerchief

Mill
They is coming from the second H'egg, which is
coming from the jar which is coming from my
H'eggshell.

Mr Hansen
My eggshell

Mill pauses and looks at Mr Hansen.

You gave the egg to me.
It was my eggshell.
My jar, my second egg and my coins.

He takes the coins back from Mill.

Mill looks bemused.

Mr Hansen stands up.

Good evening to you all

Mr Hansen walks out.

There is a short silence after he has gone.

Mill

Now see what you is done
Bill, he is taken my coins
I is never had coins before

Mill runs to the door and watches him go.

Francis starts to leave.

Bill

Wait you

Francis

Why?

Bill

What is he about?
What is he doing?

Francis

What?

Bill

Here?
Why is he come here?

Francis looks perplexed. He starts to speak, then changes his mind.

Be telling me I'm wrong
Francis
Be telling me he isn't here to bring his business
Be telling me that Francis
That you and he . . .

Francis

Is a surprise.

Bill

No

Francis

He told me not to tell you yet

Pause.

> Yes
> Is a factory
> A factory Aunty Mill
> Right here on the island

Bill

> No Francis, can't be
> We is got nothing
> What is we got that he could be wanting?

Francis

> Crawfish
> Crawfish
> Crawfish from our island
> To put in his jars.

SCENE THREE

At dusk the same day. By the shore.

Rebecca is bathing in the sea.

Francis is sitting by the water's edge, facing away from her and playing with some rocks.

Rebecca climbs out of the water behind him. She is naked and pregnant.

Francis

> Is nowhere has sand like this
> Nowhere
> Is nowhere as light
> As shiny
> As black

Francis throws them down.

> I looked for you as I stepped off the boat

Rebecca picks up a towel.

And in the village
I looked for you all over.

Rebecca starts drying herself.

I came around to your house this afternoon
I walked up and down
Everywhere

Rebecca
Stop

Francis
Have you missed me?
Missed me missed me?
I thought about you
All the time
What you were doing, what you were thinking

Rebecca
Be turning
Francis be turning around
Look at me

Francis does so.

He sees her pregnant stomach for the first time.

Pause.

Rebecca starts to put on her clothes.

I was telling you not to go
Time and time I was telling you
Stay with me I was saying
Stay with me
Don't go
I know, you don't need to be telling me again
I was hearing it at the time
You was needing to go
That's what you said
You was needing to go

Rebecca laughs.

> You was needing to go
> Like the reading and numbers and all those things
>   you was needing to do
> Needing to
> Well you is been now. Isn't you?

She picks up her stuff and starts to walks away.

Francis

> They hated me
> Rebecca?
> They hated me
> Everywhere I went they . . .
> They said I talked funny
> I dressed like . . .
> I didn't know what CUNT meant
> Do you know what CUNT is meaning?
> They played a trick on me
> Pretended they were my friend then . . .
> The men I was working with they . . .
> And every time I did something or said something
> In my stupid island way of talking.
> I kept a piece of glass in my pocket
> Here against my leg
> A broken piece of a jar
> That could cut deep.
> And every time I got it wrong or forgot
> I turned it
> Further and further in.

Rebecca

> Francis . . .

Rebecca is more gentle now.

Francis

> Do you know what CUNT means Rebecca?
> Oh yes, of course you know

Of course you do
CUNT and SCREW and FUCK and all those words
You know all about it

Rebecca starts to walk off.

Francis calls after her.

I love you.

Then more quietly after she is gone:

I love you.

SCENE FOUR

The middle of the same night. Mill and Bill's house.

Bill is having a sleepless night and is fully dressed in his outdoor clothes.

He stands in the kitchen, surrounded by three large sacks of potatoes.

He empties the sacks on to the floor, and starts dividing the potatoes one by one into seven smaller piles, muttering seven surnames as he goes (Rodgers, Repetto, Hagan, Glass, Green, Lavarello, Swain).

Mill comes down in her night dress.

She watches him without saying anything. Then,

Mill
Bill?

Bill
Back to bed

Mill
They's the seeding potatoes

Bill carries on muttering.

Who is these piles for?

Bill

Back to bed with you

Mill

Bill?

You is giving away our crop?

He goes around the piles adding one as he passes. Mill comes and gets in his way.

Bill

I's making my will

Pause.

Mill

What?

Bill stops and considers.

He decides to say something, then changes his mind.

He puts another couple of potatoes down.

He stops for a second.

Bill

Is all bad Mill

I don't like it

Mill

Tch

Bill

They is told me

Mill

Who?

Bill

The Old Hands

Mill

What?

Bill
Is when they is saved me. Before when I is drowning
    because the water is juddering.
They is come and pull me out.
Watch out for the water
Watch out for the water, they is saying
The water is turning

Mill
The only thing turning is you William Lavarello
Is turning soft in the head

Pause.

Bill
I is only known the water go like this once before Mill

Pause.

Mill
You is always been the sensible one
You is the one that is always told me not to pay any
    heed to this or to that
Don't be getting any ideas you is always saying

Bill starts dividing his potatoes again.

Mill
Bill . . . stop this
You is scaring me

Bill
I's just being prepared Mill

Mill
Please . . .
Please stop Bill

She puts her hands over her ears.

Bill
Was like the time before

Mill
    Bill
    You and me is going to make old bones.
    Old old bones
    We is going to be living in this little house of ours,
        with our potatoes and our patches until we is one
        hundred and ten.
    One hundred and ten
    Is no need to be making a will for a long while yet
    Remember what we is used to saying when we was
        young?

Bill nods reluctantly.

    So is all alright then.

Mill comes and puts an arm around him.

    We is going to be alright
    We is all going to be just fine

Bill looks at the piles of potatoes.

Mill starts picking them up and putting them back into the bag they came from.

Bill
    I wish Francis hadn't gone to Cape Town

Mill
    Is nothing to do with Francis

Bill
    Only like this one time before.
    Only like this once.

Francis walks in.

Silence.

He sits down at the table.

Mill goes to Francis and gives him a kiss.

Mill
    Is lovely to have you back love
    You is needing to be taking care of this uncle you is got
    His mind be playing tricks again

Mill leaves.

Bill is awkward in front of Francis.

He isn't sure now whether to carry on with his will or not.

He brings over a pile of potatoes and puts them down in front of Francis.

Bill
    You look after them well
    They is good ones
    And is a patch
    Is your name on it

Francis
    Why?

Bill shrugs.

Francis indicates the piles of potatoes on the floor.

    What is all this for?

Bill starts putting the potatoes away.

Bill
    Up to bed lad

Pause.

Bill continues putting the potatoes away.

Francis
    Did you know about Rebecca?

Beat.

Bill
    Yes

Francis

You didn't tell me

Beat.

Bill

We wasn't sure . . .

Pause.

Francis

Expect everyone blames me
Is that right?
What did I expect, going off to Cape Town?
Leaving her by herself?

Bill doesn't answer.

To think I missed you all
Even you
I even missed you.

Pause.

Bill

Is no one blaming you

Francis fiddles with the plates on the table.

Francis

Anyway she'll be sorry
One day when she sees
She'll be sorry

Pause.

Bill can't decide whether to say anything or not, finally blurts out:

Bill

Be careful with this Mr Hansen, Francis
You need to be careful

So you met him in Cape Town, doesn't mean you
  knows him

Pause.

Does it?
We isn't knowing anything about him
He could be anyone

He turns around to look at Francis.

Oh I knows he's very clever
I isn't denying that
But I isn't so sure about him
I isn't trusting him
Come here and do fancy magic
So what? Is meaning nothing
Is not so good
Isn't magic
Is a trick
And is you he's tricking
This factory idea is . . .
Is no good Francis
Is no good

Francis

You don't even know what it would be like
You haven't even heard the plans

Bill

I is heard enough
I is seen enough

Francis

We is both seen

Beat.

Bill

What I is seen is in Mr Hansen's face
Right here between the eyes
I isn't liking it

49

Our island crawfish
And he is thinking money
We isn't wanting that
Our crawfish for Mr Hansen's money

Francis

Be something new
Be something to do

Bill

We isn't wanting something new

Francis

We isn't or you isn't?

Beat.

Bill

We isn't

Francis

NO
You isn't
They'll be saying yes
They'll be loving it
It's you
Is you that is frightened

Beat.

Bill

Is nothing wrong with being frightened Francis
We isn't like Cape Town here

Francis

Anyway it isn't up to you
You is just given me a patch

Bill

Still will be needing to go to the vote
Everyone is having a say

Francis

So is up to everyone

Bill

    Everyone? Yes,
    After everyone has asked everyone what they is
        thinking
    And this everyone is asked that everyone
    And that everyone is asked the next everyone
    And the next and the next
    Until no one is made up their minds, Francis.
    They is all just watching see what everyone else is
        doing,
    Then someone is looking at me.
    What is Bill saying, they is asking?
    What is Bill saying?
    And then they is all asking what is Bill saying?
    What is Bill saying? What is Bill saying?
    And maybe if I could be saying Yes, and meaning Yes
    Then everyone is saying Yes,
    The Yes and we is having this factory
    But
    If I is saying No
    And meaning No . . .

Beat.

Francis

    No one tried to stop you
    Twenty years ago, no one tried to stop you
    When you came back from Cape Town and had this
        great idea
    Build a church
    No one said anything
    You didn't have to go to the vote
    Ask everyone if they wanted it
    You just went straight in and did it

Bill

    Was different then
    We needed it

Francis

> Took everyone up to the lake
> Baptised the whole island in a single day
> No questions then

Bill

> We was needing it

Francis

> Taught us things, read us things, told us stories, all
>   those stories, on Sundays about the bible
> Did you ask any of us?

Beat.

Bill

> Is you ever seen a dog eat a man Francis?
> Seen bodies is strewn like . . .
> Of course you isn't
> I is glad you isn't
> But I is seen it
> H'out there
> H'outside
> When I was there
> They was having a name for it
> They was saying there is reasons
> Complicated reasons
> Is 'war' they is called it
> Was country against country
> Is to do with armies
> But it was dogs. Dogs chewing dead mens
> But whatever has been done out there
> I is seen just as bad done here
> Oh maybe is not bodies strewn
> And maybe is not dogs
> Maybe is not war
> But is as bad

Pause.

We was needing a church but we isn't needing a
    factory.

Francis
    I don't believe you
    Dogs don't eat men

Bill
    I saw them

Francis
    No
    You are just saying this to stop me

Bill
    No, I isn't wanting to stop you
    Just is wanting you to be thinking

Beat.

    What will the factory be bringing?
    What do we need, that we isn't got?
    Here we is working for ourselves
    You is wanting us all to be working for Mr Hansen
        for the rest of our days?

Francis
    Is better than just being stuck with the mountain and
        the patches

Beat.

Bill
    Alright

Bill comes and sits next to Francis.

    Take it to the vote
    Tell them about your idea
    Be letting them make up their minds
    Be doing and saying what you want to persuade them
    I won't be saying a thing
    Neither way

Not a word.
You can be taking it to the vote and I won't even be
    raising my hand

Pause,

If you is doing something for me
If.
Is only on condition you is doing this thing
Isn't for me, is for you,
Is for all of us
Is just a little thing
Be going up to the mountain first thing in the morning
Be standing at the pool
Be washing yourself in the water, Francis
Walking right in until is up to your waist
Be putting your head down under the surface
And listen
Just be listening
Is all
You listen
You see what you can hear
Then you'll be knowing whether is right or not
You decide

Pause.

Is up to you lad
Is all up to you now
I is going to bed

Bill walks up the stairs.

SCENE FIVE

The following morning.

*Rebecca is sitting by herself on a patch of land,
overlooking the sea.*

Mill and Mr Hansen arrive. Mill sits down a little distance away from Rebecca.

Mill
Be running along Rebecca.

Rebecca doesn't move.

Be running along, we is sitting here

Rebecca
I is sitting here

Mill
And so is we
You can be sitting somewhere else now
Go on
We is busy here
Be sitting Mr Hansen

Mill pats the ground beside her.

Mr Hansen sits.

Rebecca doesn't move.

Said move
We is waiting on something important

Rebecca
So is I

Mill
What is you waiting on?

Rebecca
The sea

Mill
The sea is always here
Along with you girl
You be waiting for the sea someplace farther along

Or go and be smiling at the sailors on the boat, why
don't you?
Go and be smiling at the sailors like you is done before

Rebecca
I is never smiled at no sailors
NEVER.

Rebecca moves off.

NEVER NEVER

*Mill watches her go, then says to Mr Hansen after she is
gone,*

Mill
Well is must have been smiling at someone

*Mr Hansen is nervous, he is tapping his foot on the
ground.*

They won't be long

Mr Hansen
They've been hours

Mill
They'll be out soon
When is the boat be leaving?

Mr Hansen
Tomorrow

Mill
They'll be out by then

Pause.

Be telling me again

Mr Hansen
What?

Mill
I likes hearing

Mr Hansen
No, my mind's busy

Mr Hansen paces up and down a bit.

Mill
Change your mind of it

Mr Hansen sits down with a sigh. He gets a jar out of his pocket.

Mr Hansen
I don't know where to begin

Mill
With the machines,
Machines you and Francis is going to build

Mr Hansen stands up, he takes a few steps.

Mr Hansen
The machines will go about here

Mill
Here or here?

Mr Hansen
There

Mill
How many?

Mr Hansen
Five to begin with

Mill
Then maybe six

Mr Hansen
Then maybe six

Mill
What will they be looking like?

Mr Hansen
Big

Mill
And delicate
With great long knives

Mr Hansen
Like great . . .

Mill
Flapping birds
And where is I going to be?

Mr Hansen
You'll be here
Some of you. Standing along here

Mill
Dressing like this?

Mr Hansen
No, wearing uniform

Mill
Is wearing my H'uniform
You's forgetting the buttons

Mr Hansen
Each of you will have a panel in front of you

Mill
With buttons

Mr Hansen
With buttons

Mill
And when we is pressing the buttons, the machine
goes . . .

Mr Hansen
It comes on

Mill switches the imaginary button and the imaginary machine comes on.

Mill
Goes brrr
But what is here?

Mr Hansen
You tell me

Mill
No, you do the saying

Mr Hansen
You know as well as I do.

Mill
I want you to be saying.

Mr Hansen
Well when the chopped crayfish go out of the machines, which they do about here . . .

Mill
Or here, is depending whether we is having five or six . . .

Mr Hansen
They'll be carried along.

Mill
On this thing, is like a belt but isn't a belt, is much bigger, and moving, and will go right the way along, right here.

Mr Hansen
Until . . .

Mill
Poof.

Mr Hansen
Comes out here.

Mill

In the jar-ing room,
Where we is all standing in a line.

Mr Hansen

And will put the pieces into the jars.

Mill

Only not any-old-how, but carefully so is same
amount in each.
But where is Francis?

Mr Hansen

Francis?

Mill

He's being the controller.

Mr Hansen

Then he's in the controller's room.

Mill

With the glass window?

Mr Hansen

A glass window so he can watch the machines.

Mill

And us.

Mr Hansen

And you.

Mill

And if we is doing something wrong?

Mr Hansen

He'll tap on the glass.

Mill

And when the bell is going?

Mr Hansen

You'll stop.

Mill

Be turning the machines off first.

Mr Hansen

Of course.

Mill

Pushing the buttons, say stop, the machine is going . . .
    nothing
Is stopped
Then we is taking off the H'uniform, is walking along
    here . . . .
To here
Here is where we is sitting
Eating our lunch

Mr Hansen

We'll build a canteen for you

Mill

Canteen?

Mr Hansen

A place to eat lunch

Mill

We'll be sitting in our canteen
And the name of the factory is saying 'Mr Hansen
    and Francis'

Mr Hansen

Just Hansen

Mill

What about Francis?

Mr Hansen

He'll have his name inside

Mill

On his desk?

Mr Hansen
Yes

Mill
Behind the glass?

Mr Hansen
Yes

Mill
In the controller's room?

Mr Hansen
Yes

Mill
Say 'Francis Swain,
Controller'

She mimes this.

Mr Hansen sits down.

You can't be sitting down, you has to do the talking

Mr Hansen
You've said it all

Mill
No I hasn't. You be saying more

Mr Hansen
I'm tired

Mill
I'm tired
I's been filling all the jars

Mr Hansen
Come and sit down then

Mill
In the canteen?

Mr Hansen
Yes

Mill sits down in the canteen.

Mill
I is made you a cup of tea if you want one

Mr Hansen
Thank you

Mill
Come and drink it then

Mr Hansen goes over and sits beside her.

She gives him a mimed cup. He takes it and nearly drinks but then comes to his senses.

Mill notices his anxiety.

They'll be along soon

Mr Hansen gets up again and looks at his watch.

You know I is thinking the canteen be better over the other side

He looks at her.

Be getting a better view of the sea is all

Mr Hansen
Here they come

Mr Hansen jumps up.

Mill finishes her mimed cup of tea and stays where she is at first.

Francis and Bill walk back.

Neither man says anything.

Well, go on.

Pause.

Bill
Is off
Over

Mr Hansen
What?

Francis
Is right

Mr Hansen
They voted it out?

Bill
No
They voted it in
They loved the idea

Mr Hansen
I don't understand

Francis
I voted it out

Mr Hansen
Why?
Francis?

Francis
I'm sorry

Mr Hansen
I don't understand

Bill
Is needing to be getting back to your other concerns
now I suppose Mr Hansen

Mr Hansen
I need an explanation

Mill
What is going on here?

Mill leaves her tea and comes over.

Bill
There isn't going to be any factory

Mill
Why not?

Bill
Francis is changed his mind

Mill
Can he be doing that?

Bill
Is done

Mill
What about the canteen and the H'uniform?

Francis
I'm sorry Mr Hansen

Mr Hansen
You said there would be no problem

Bill
They'll be no canteen now

Francis
I didn't think there would be . . . I . . .

Mill
No H'uniform?

Mr Hansen
I came all this way

Francis
I know

Bill
Come on Mill
They is needing to talk

Mill

No jar-ing room?

Francis

Here,

I'm sorry

Francis gives Mr Hansen back the briefcase.

Mr Hansen

What, so that is it?

Final?

Over?

No more discussion?

Do you know how many miles I have travelled Francis?

How much time I have put into this?

How much . . .

God I was a fool to have ever even thought

Look at you, you're a kid, a lad

Just a lad

To even have met you was

Alright

So it is over

Finis

Gone

End of a dream

Island crayfish, no longer

But what about my time?

Time is money Francis?

What about all the money I spent?

You can't do this to people

Not without an explantion

You just changed your mind?

That's crap

Sorry Mrs Lavarello, but it's crap

Bill

You can be telling him more than that, can't you?

Be telling him what you saw

Mill
What?

Bill
He is heard something
Is heard something in the water Mr Hansen
Is gone to the lake Mill
Early this morning is what he is said
Francis?

Mr Hansen
Enough is enough
He heard something?
This I don't believe

Bill
Tell him Francis
Yes, in the water

Mr Hansen
No.
Sorry
I've had it
I'm not interested any more
This is business Mr Lavarello, not some . . .
I don't care what he heard or saw
I'm going back to the ship

Francis
I'm sorry Mr Hansen

Mr Hansen looks about the island. He sniffs the air.

Mr Hansen
No
I'm the sorry one
It is still a beautiful island

He gives the briefcase to Mill.

You keep this.
Who knows?
Maybe you'll need it some day

He takes a jar out of his pocket and gives it to Francis.

And you
See if you can turn it back into an egg

Bill

We have plenty H'eggs

Mr Hansen

Use it to store them in then

Mr Hansen leaves.

Francis sits down heavily. He looks at the jar.

Bill

Is right you is a lad, but you is a good lad

Mill

Francis?

Francis doesn't respond; he looks at Mill.

Francis

When I was in Cape Town he was my only friend.

Bill

Be standing up lad
You is done a good thing
Is really good to be having you home
Isn't it Mill?
Is really good to be having him home

Mill

Is all in favour yesterday
Is thinking is a good idea

Bill

That was yesterday wasn't it Francis?

Francis

I is sorry Mill

Bill

Is no reason to be sorry
Is done a good thing, is no reason to be sorry

Mill

Is you really seen the water, Francis?

Pause.

Bill

Of course he is seen it
Anyone be seeing it if they went up there
You be telling her Francis

Francis

NO.
Stop Uncle Bill
Is nothing shaking

Bill

But you said you saw . . .

Francis

I didn't see anything
If I is said I did, I is said it to shut you up was all.

Bill

You is lying
He is lying Mill, don't listen
Is lying

Mill

Hush now Bill

Bill

NO.
Tell her.
Be telling her the truth

Francis

You're trapped, Uncle Bill
It is all mixed up in your mind
You built your church,
You is made the island the way you want
But now it is trapping you

Pause.

I'm sorry Aunty Mill
But I is made a decision
Was a mistake to think I could be living here again
Here?
I don't know what I was thinking
I'm going to go back to Cape Town with Mr Hansen

Pause.

I'll leave with the boat.

Mill

Francis, no?

Francis

There is nothing for me here any more Aunty Mill

Francis looks from one to another.

I had better get my stuff together,
Catch Mr Hansen.
I . . .
Aunty Mill?
I am not a lad.

He puts the jar that Mr Hansen gave him down into the sand.

Mill

Francis . . .?

Francis walks away, leaving Bill and Mill in silence.

Go after him Bill.

Bill doesn't move.

Go after him

Bill
He did see . . .

Mill
No, Bill
Not one more word
We is always losing everything
Everything is always being taken away from us
Not Francis
Francis is all that we ever had
Is all left, Bill
Go after him
Change his mind of it
Quick

Pause.

Bill
It wasn't just the wind. He did hear . . .

Mill
BILL

Pause.

Why is you not going after him? Oh, yes, I is
forgetting, you is never cared for Francis. Just
be standing back watching him go. Say 'Goodbye
Francis – on you go'? As easy as that, because is
Swain. Isn't Lavarello so you is pleased to see
him go.

Bill
Isn't true Mill.
His mind is made is all.
Won't be anything I can be saying to change it

Mill

Well maybe you is going to watch him go
But I isn't
No.
Is not saying goodbye to Francis

Bill

What is you meaning?

Mill

If Francis is leaving
He's not the only one on that boat be waving you
goodbye

Beat.

If Francis is leaving this island tomorrow then I'm
having to be leaving with him

Beat.

Bill

NO
No Mill
Don't say that.
You isn't knowing what you are saying

Mill

I'm meaning it Bill
Not Francis

Bill

But . . .
You and me, we is . . .
Please Mill
Is no way I can be making him stay Mill
He is never listening to me

Mill

Then tomorrow you and I is saying goodbye.

Bill
But is Old Bones, Mill?

Mill
No
Not without Francis
Is no life here for me without Francis

Bill

Pause.

Mill?

Mill
I is meaning it Bill.
Francis goes and I go.

She stands up. She looks at Bill, then leaves.

SCENE SIX

The same day. Rebecca's house.

Bill arrives at Rebecca's front door. Rebecca answers it.

Rebecca
Oh.

Bill
Can I come in?

Rebecca
Is no one here

Bill
Is you I is come to see

Rebecca
Me?

She opens the door. Bill walks in and sits down at the table.

If Francis is sent you I is not interested in hearing

Bill

Francis isn't sent me

Rebecca

Oh.

Pause.

Rebecca looks about her.

Is no tea.
No milk
Cow is on strike
Isn't eating
Isn't moving
Is giving no milk for four days
So don't be asking me for tea

Rebecca sits.

She is trying her best to be polite.

If you want water I can be taking it from the stream

Bill

No
No water.

Pause.

Rebecca

So, what is you wanting?

Bill doesn't answer.

Is you sure you is come to see me?
No one is ever come to see me.

Bill

Francis is leaving

Rebecca doesn't answer.

Tomorrow
Is leaving with the boat

Pause.

Has you heard?

Rebecca nods.

Rebecca
Why?

Bill
Lots of reasons
And you
You and lots of reasons

Pause.

Rebecca
Francis is never doing anything because of me

Pause.

Bill
Is never coming back
You know that?
Not never
He goes and none of us is ever seeing him again

Rebecca
Francis makes up his own mind
Doesn't listen to no one else

Bill
Francis has always had a mind that could make itself
    up
But is not only Francis
Milly
Is saying she will be going too
My Milly
Is saying she is going where Francis goes
Oh and she is meaning it

Is all ready to be stepping on that boat, wave me off
as it disappears
And once Mill is leaving, then the next person be
leaving
And then the next is leaving
And then the next and the next . . .

Rebecca
Mr Lavarello,
Is nothing to do with me.

She stands up.

Bill
Say the child is his

Pause.

Then a second pause as Rebecca realises that Bill

means it.

Rebecca
Is a lie

Bill
I know

Rebecca
You is asking me to lie?
You?

Bill shrugs.

Pause.

Is impossible anyway

Bill
Impossible?

Rebecca
Impossible Francis is the father

Bill
Impossible or unlikely?

Rebecca
Impossible

Pause.

Unless you isn't counting right

Bill
Francis isn't able to count

Rebecca
Yes he is

Bill
Not very well

Rebecca
Francis is able to count very well indeed

Bill
But he won't

Rebecca
He might

Bill
Be taking the risk, Rebecca
Please

Pause.

Rebecca has a hard look at Bill.

Rebecca
You always was telling us lies is wrong

Bill
I know

Rebecca
All my life you is telling us . . .

77

Bill
I know

Pause.

Rebecca
No
I isn't going to
I couldn't be doing it
Not for ever
For ever and ever

Bill
He is wanting it to be
Very badly
He would stay and . . .
You and he . . .

Rebecca
No no no
Stop saying this

Bill
Has you already told the someone else?

Rebecca
No

Bill
So why is you crying?

Pause.

Bill stands up.

I is sorry I has troubled you

Bill starts to leave.

I'll see you tomorrow
At the shore

Beat.

You are a good girl Rebecca

Rebecca
No
I is not
I's bad
You don't know me.
I's bad.
Very very bad

Bill
I should not be troubling you

Rebecca
I isn't wanting Francis to leave

Bill
I know

Rebecca
Don't be going just yet
Be . . .
Be letting me think
Be letting me . . .
I can't, I . . .
If I said yes,
If I was saying yes
Is only if
If I is saying yes, what would you do?
Would you be doing anything?
Would you be surprised?
Is you thinking I won't?
Definitely
Because I might,
I might just
I might
If I did, what would you be doing?

Bill
Cry

Just for joy
Francis be staying and my Mill

Rebecca
Is nothing
Crying
Anyone can cry
I can cry
I can cry by myself
Don't need to say lies to cry

Beat.

What else would you be doing?

Beat.

Bill
What is you wanting?

Rebecca laughs.

Rebecca
No
Not what I is wanting
Is what you is wanting
Nobody is caring what I want
Nobody is even knowing what I want

Bill
What do you want?

Rebecca
I want this baby dead

Beat.

There, I is said it
I is wanting this baby dead
The second this baby is born
As soon as it is breathing
The very second, I want someone to be picking it up,
Like this and turning it round and holding it down,

Hard, its face in the sand,
And to keep holding and holding it down so hard.
Until . . .

Pause.

Bill
Rebecca . . . I

Rebecca
See I is told you I is bad
Bad bad.

Bill
You is wanting someone to kill your child?

Rebecca
Is not my child
I is just the carrier
I's just like a ship is carrying it

Pause.

I know
I know you is saying that you can't
You can't
Of course you can't
Is obvious you can't

Beat.

But I is thinking you could
Just
Just for a minute, maybe, you could
That was all
If you was wanting to badly enough
And I know you is wanting me to say yes very bad
I was thinking that maybe, you could
You could maybe . . .
Could you?

SCENE SEVEN

Bill by the water.

He should not move to the water but be suddenly surrounded by it.

He is up to his waist again, and the deafening juddering is all around.

He shouts out 'What are you?'
Silence.

SCENE EIGHT

A few days later.

Mill and Francis, inside Mill's house.

It is exactly the same as the start of the Act, apart from a cloth on the table, and a general feeling that it has been prettied.

Francis has just entered.

Mill is calm.

Mill
Been waiting
Since the sun is first up
Been watching through the chinks in the roof as up
    it came
Been holding my breath as the hours go by

Francis
Mill . . .

Mill
Don't touch me
Stay where you are
I's wanting to see you first

Other way
You'll not be coming back to visit I suppose now
You'll be like a stranger to the pair of us
You won't will you, Francis?

Francis

No

Mill

Oh you may be as thinking you won't but you isn't
    knowing
You'll be getting busy and forgetting all about us

Francis

I'll be less than a mile.

Mill

Ah but I is remembering my mother saying this to
    my sister and she is saying 'No' but ding, the day
    she is marrying that is it, she is only coming back
    for Christmases and one Sunday a month and she
    is only living up the stairs.

Francis

I'll be coming back to visit

Mill

And then is the baby
You won't be having time when the baby is come
Should have been telling me it was your baby Francis,
All these months of seeing Rebecca be growing and
    was your baby
Be turning again
Turning and turning
Is suiting you this suit
Is worn by my father, and your father
You is knowing that?
And Uncle Bill the day we is got wed
All of them is wearing this
And I is worn the wedding dress Rebecca be wearing
We is all worn it

Oh sure, never be the same again now Rebecca is
worn it, is had to put three extra pieces up the side,
but still . . .
Maybe you is best standing on your toes because
those trousers is far too long at the bottom

Francis stands up on his toes.

Is much better

Francis
Bill isn't even spoke to me

Mill
He doesn't mean it
Is all over Francis
Mr Hansen is two days gone
Is all over by now

Francis drops down again.

No, be staying like that
You must be staying like that Francis
Have you got a flower?

Francis
Is no flowers at this time of year

Mill
You must be having a flower Francis
They is all had flowers

Francis
Mill?

*Mill looks to the wall of magazine cuttings. She gets
down a picture of a flower as if picking it from her
garden.*

Mill
Everyone who is married is having flower
No complaining Francis

Mill fusses putting the magazin flower into his lapel.

Francis
I saw everyone

Mill
Hmm?

Francis
Waiting
I didn't know you had told them all to wait

Mill
Where?

Francis
Out there, waiting for my wedding

Mill
I didn't tell them

Francis
Of course you did
They're all standing on the shore
In a long line

Mill
Nothing to do with me

Francis
They're not waiting for me?

Mill
No

Francis
They must be waiting for something

Mill
I suppose they must

Mill has finished putting the flower into Francis's lapel.
She admires her handiwork

Is looking lovely now
Rebecca won't be knowing you
When is she coming?

Francis

Soon
Actually is past the hour

Mill

Is taking her time getting ready is all.
Maybe she is in the crowd

Francis

Why would she be in the crowd?

Mill

I don't know
Just an idea

Francis

Is her wedding day

Mill

I know

Francis

Why would she be standing in the crowd on her
    wedding day?

Mill

I don't know

Francis

And why is the crowd standing out there anyway?
Waiting?
What is they waiting for?
The crowd is never standing outside like that on a
    wedding day
Just looking
Should be standing in the church

Mill
Maybe is a boat coming

Francis
We is just had a boat

Mill
Or a storm
Was hearing thunder before

Francis
Maybe I will go up to her house
See where she is

Mill
Maybe she is forgotten the time
Is not so late
Few moments is all

Francis
I don't like them standing out there
Looking

Francis starts to go.

Mill
We'll be meeting you at the church, will we?
Be coming back here love, give me another kiss

Mill kisses Francis.

I is proud of you,
You know that?
Very proud.

Francis leaves.

Mill goes over and shouts up the stairs.

Bill?
Is you ready Bill?
Bill?
Is Francis' wedding day and you is supposed to be at
the church already

Bill comes down the stairs.

Bill

Is wonderful Mill
Is wonderful
Is so . . .

He takes her by the hands and swings her around.

I is been standing on the roof
Is beautiful and extraordinary
Come and be looking
Come come

Mill

You isn't even dressed

Bill

Isn't the water Mill
Isn't the water
And isn't my mind
Is the mountain underneath

Mill

What is you talking about?

Bill

I is seen it this morning
I is followed smoke up the mountain
Is great clouds of smoke
Coloured clouds, colours you is never seen
Pinks, reds, greens
And I is seen it
Is boiling now, is really boiling
Is coming up in bubbles of red red hot
So hot is burning your eyes to look at it
And steam and under the mountain is fire
Great arms of fire coming out, is like a little flower
    with great arms
Go to the window Mill, be seeing for yourself
Quick

Mill
  Bill?

Bill
  Look Mill, be standing at the window
  Was you ever seeing such a . . .

Mill looks over to the window. She moves to have a better view.

Mill
  Is hot?

Bill
  Is so hot, would melt the moon

Mill looks again.

Mill
  What about our houses?

Bill doesn't answer.

  Don't want all those colours and fire and boiling
    coming here

Bill shakes his head.

Bill
  Is miles away
  Is at the top of the mountain.
  Is not coming here

Mill looks again.

Mill
  You is sure?

Bill
  I think it might be God, Mill

He gives her a kiss on both cheeks.

  I think this might be God
  After all this time . . .
  I think this might be

Francis comes back in.

Mill

Where's Rebecca?

Francis

Is not coming
She . . . .
Is the baby
Her baby is started
She is screaming and crying
Our baby has started coming

Mill

Oh my goodness

Francis

She is clutching herself here and saying she is ripping
apart

Mill

Who is with her?

Francis

No one

Mill

What?

Francis

I's frightened Mill

Mill

Wait a minute, I'll go

Francis

No. She doesn't want anyone

Mill

She may be saying that but . . .

Francis

She sent me away
She doesn't want anyone there

No one
She is saying that she wants to be alone
She is only asking for one person

Mill

Who?

Francis

Him.
You, Uncle Bill
She is asking for you.

The sound of juddering returns.

Bill picks up his jumper and walks out.

Mill and Francis watch him, motionless.

The juddering gets louder and with it is the sound of the islanders' pandemonium and panic. A woman's piercing scream is heard and this continues after the other sounds have stopped.

SCENE NINE

On top of the screaming a pounding is heard.

Francis is pounding at the door of Rebecca's house, and shouting her name.

He is half hysterical and very weary. Eventually Mill comes beside him.

Mill

Come on now Francis.
Come on.
Let's be going.

She leads him away.

SCENE TEN

The following dawn, with all its calm.

The immediate tremors from the mountain have stopped.

Rebecca is standing alone in her house.

She is wearing a slip and holding a wedding dress in her arms. It is covered in blood.

In front of her is a bucket of water that she uses to try and wash off the blood.

She stands up, and moves to a rocking chair and tries to sit down.

All her movements are slow; she is very sore and also in shock.

Bill enters. He stands beside her.

Neither of them say anything.

Rebecca starts to rock the chair very slowly.

Rebecca
Let's play a game, the sailors said

Bill stands at her side, shattered.

Pause.

Come aboard, the sailors said

She rocks a little more.

Play a game
The sailors said

Bill
Was a girl

Rebecca
A game
Play . . .

Bill

A tiny tiny little girl

Pause.

Rebecca hears this but doesn't show any reaction.

Rebecca

Play a game they said
A game

Pause.

So I was playing, and they was playing
On the big ship that was come
Three of them
And me
Playing
And laughing and laughing and
Harder and harder
Until I . . .
Until I isn't wanting to . . .
I isn't wanting to play any more
And I is telling them stop
Stop I is saying
Stop stop
Please stop
But they's playing on
And on
And on
And on
Until . . .
I . . .

Rebecca starts rocking again.

She forces herself to think of something else.

Bill lets out a long horrible howl that has welled up from inside.

He crumples.

Rebecca doesn't know what to do but puts a hand on his shoulders.

He moves in towards her and holds on to her legs, desperate.

Rebecca doesn't move.

Bill
It was . . .

Rebecca
Shouldn't have ever even been . . .

Pause.

You must be . . .
Be standing
Is something is gone now
Is over
Is gone
Wasn't a baby
Was a thing should never have been born . . .

She helps him up.

He is more fragile than she is.

Bill
Saw something good today

Rebecca doesn't know what to say.

I . . .

He turns to her.

Was in the mountain
Was good, all good.

Bill suddenly realises.

Isn't baptised
Rebecca?

Is unbaptised
We can't . . .

Someone knocks impatiently three times on the door.

They both freeze.

Bill tries to turn around, confused.

Is no one born on the island that is unbaptised

More knocking.

Rebecca
Mr Lavarello
Stand up
Please
You is going to have to stand up

The knocking continues.

They is going to come in
We is going to have to let them in

Bill goes off to one of the other rooms.

Still more knocks.

What is you doing?
You . . .

Bill returns with the baby wrapped up in a blanket.

Rebecca looks on horrified.

Bill bends down and takes some of the water from the bucket in his hand.

He unwraps the baby's head and baptises it.

Bill
In the name of the Father, Son and Holy Ghost I is
baptising you . . .

He looks at Rebecca.

Rebecca can hardly speak.

Rebecca
I isn't . . . .
Anything
Please
I isn't . . .
Misfortune

Bill
Misfortune.

He covers the head up again, very gently.

Misfortune

Pause.

Again there is more knocking.

Pause.

Bill holds on to the baby, and speaks so quietly he almost doesn't make a sound at all.

Misfortune
Misfortune

Rebecca slowly goes to the door and opens it.

Mill and Mr Hansen are on the other side.

Mill comes in first. She sees the situation and stops.

She is followed by Mr Hansen.

Mr Hansen is carrying a large wide-beamed torch, and wearing a protective coat.

Mr Hansen
For goodness sake.
What are you doing here?
You should have left long ago – everyone's gone
    already.
They're all on the ship, waiting for you.

Rebecca

Where's Francis?

Mr Hansen

On the ship.
I told you.
And the ship must leave. It's too dangerous.
You have to move.

Beat.

The island's been evacuated
You're the only two left.
The volcano could go off again at any moment.
If you don't come now I will have to tell the ship
to leave
NOW, Mr Lavarello.

Bill

The baby is dead

Mr Hansen stops.

Mr Hansen

I'm sorry

Pause.

Bill

And I is done it

Pause. Mr Hansen doesn't know what to say, he isn't even sure he understands.

I is killed it

Beat.

And now we is needing to . . .
We is needing to bury it

Bill turns around to face Rebecca, with some new energy.

We can't just be leaving it

Mr Hansen
Mr Lavarello you don't understand, you . . .

Bill
We is needing to bury her

Mr Hansen is too shocked and out of his depth to add anything.

I'll be taking it to the church
Is a vault
Was made when we built it

Mr Hansen
You can't get near the church
It's cut off
They've put up tape
It isn't safe

Bill starts to move with the baby.

Bill
I is going to try

Mr Hansen
Mr Lavarello you . . .

Mr Hansen physically stands in his path.

I can't let you
You'll be killed
Give me the baby, we can take it back to the boat

Bill
NO

Bill snatches it away.

They are in stalemate, neither person will let the other near.

Mill steps out of the shadows and takes charge of the situation.

Mill
I'll take it

I'll take them both
All three of them to the church
I is knowing a way is not taped off.

She holds out her arms for the baby.

Bill gives it to her.

She starts to walk out.

Bill and Rebecca follow her, suddenly like small children.

Mill (*to Mr Hansen*)

You is coming with us
And after . . .
We is coming back to the ship
Straight after
Together
And when we is getting back to the ship
You isn't saying a word
Not any of this to anyone
Is you clear?
Was born dead.
Is what we will say.
Is enough shouting and screaming
Is the whole world turning upside down already
Mr Hansen?
Was born dead.
Is things about the island that you isn't understanding
You isn't saying a word.

Mill, Bill and Rebecca leave.

Mr Hansen remains, stunned.

End of Act One.

Act Two

SCENE ONE

Southampton, England. Eleven months have passed since Act One.

Inside Mr Hansen's jar factory.

Mill enters Mr Hansen's office in a flurry.

Mill
Is said I is needing an appointment.
Is said I is needing an appointment, and I is said I is
    coming in.
Is said I is needing an appointment and hah, I is said
    I isn't
Is said I is needing an appointment and I is said,
I isn't, I isn't when he is come smashing H'egg
    in our kitchen, why is I needing one now?
And is looking at me, all eyes down his nose
But I is standing firm
And is said I is needing an appointment
Is said I is needing an appointment and . . .

Mr Hansen
Hallo Mill

Mill stops.

What can I do for you?

Mill
Be telling Francis I isn't needing an appointment

Mr Hansen
Sit down Mill

Mill

Mr Hansen is a friend of mine, I is told him. Is a
friend of mine, so don't be making appointments
when a friend is visiting a friend

Mr Hansen

I'll tell him

Mill

Mr Hansen is your boss he is saying
Is all hairs slick down his face.

Mr Hansen

I'll tell him, Mill.

Pause. Mill sits down.

What is wrong?

Pause.

Mill

Everybody is getting sick

Mr Hansen

Go on

Mill

Is said we'd be back by now and . . .
We is learnt to count the seasons here.
But some of the seasons is even having their second
count
And every day the old people is saying to the young
people, 'soon soon,
We'll be going back soon.'
And the young people is saying to the children,
'soon soon.'
And the children is saying it to the old,
'soon.'
And everyone is looking out of the window, always
looking out of the window, and the government
men is saying 'soon'

And people in shops, and even you is saying 'soon'
And I am here to be asking when?
When Mr Hansen?
You is said we is going back, but when?

Pause.

Mr Hansen

Maybe you should have made an appointment.

Mill

We is friends isn't we? You and me? You said we was
friends.

Pause.

Is it money? I know we is expensive and everyone is
always bringing us things, and everybody be
thinking those people from the island, is better if
they never come.

Mr Hansen

It's not money

Mill

So maybe you is worried about who will be doing
our jobs? Who'll be packing all the jars when we
is gone?

Mr Hansen

It's not the jobs Mill

Mill

Or the houses, maybe you is not sure who be living
in the houses . . .

Pause.

Mr Hansen looks at his watch.

Mr Hansen

I've got a meeting, any minute.
I am going to have to go.

Mill
I is only asking what everyone is asking.

Pause.

What I is told Francis to be asking.

Mr Hansen brings up a chair.

You is looking tired Mr Hansen

Mr Hansen
I am tired.

Mr Hansen points to a map on the wall.

See that Mill. You see all those crosses. Seven crosses, they are mine.
Seven factories.
Small factories, I'll admit but . . .
I am a business man, first and foremost.
You have to remember that.

Pause.

I am sorry that they are sick

Mill
Francis says is only because they is not trying that they is sick.
Francis says they is wanting to be sick.
Francis is saying we is wanting to be complaining, be saying hah H'England is a nonsense place, is wanting to be too frightened to be going out, but isn't true.
We isn't wanting that.
We is just wanting to go home

Beat.

Mr Hansen?
Is all we want.

Mr Hansen gets his breath.

Mr Hansen
But you can't, Mill.

Beat.

I'm sorry
You can't go home
It's not possible.

Mill
Why?

Mr Hansen
Because the island has gone.

Pause.

Maybe we should have told you before, but . . .
The volcano came right up over the village, and
  buried it.

Pause.

The British Navy went out there. Quite soon after.
They sent a report to Mr Cavendish.

Mill
Nobody was telling us

Mr Hansen
We wanted you to settle in. To stop getting sick
That was the plan

Mill has to take this in.

Mill
Was Francis knowing already?

Mr Hansen
Yes.

Pause.

Mill
Is all gone?

Mr Hansen nods.

Even the meeting house? The school?

Mr Hansen
Yes

Mill
The church?

Mr Hansen
Yes

Mill
Is all gone?
Is all the houses, every single one?

Mr Hansen
Yes, Mill

Mill
Not even one left?

Mr Hansen
No

Mill
Not even my house?

Pause.

My house is gone, pff. My house is gone? Is buried,
is gone?

Mr Hansen
You have a house here.

Mill
My house is here?

Mill looks around.

So is my house here now? Is my house here, is this
house with the rain is coming through the floors?

Mr Hansen

We can do something about the damp.

Mill

No more looking out of the window and thinking
maybe is today?

Pause.

Maybe is soon soon. Is completely gone? You is sure?

Mill takes this in.

Is lucky your ship be coming to get us, then, then after
that the aeroplane, or else we is all gone.

Mill is upset, she starts to fiddle with her skirt.

But I is thinking is a shame. Is a shame about that
volcano. Is such a shame

Pause.

Is such a shame about that volcano.

Mr Hansen

I am going to have to go, Mill.
I'm sorry.

Mill nods.

You can stay in here if you want.
Take as long as you want.

Mill

Is such a shame.

Mr Hansen picks up his case.

Mr Hansen

I know

Mill

I is wishing we was still able to be looking out of the
window and think soon soon.

Mr Hansen
See, I should have waited a bit longer before telling you

Pause.

I have to go
It'll be alright Mill

Mill
Is such a shame

He touches Mill's shoulder.

Beat.

Mr Hansen
It'll be alright

He leaves.

Mill sits in silence.

Then she starts speaking slowly, almost strangulated at first.

Mill
Is no more looking out of the window
And saying is soon
Is no crawfish and Pinnawin H'eggs
Is the Queen now,
And puddings
And is no more watching weeks and weeks for a boat,
     and looking and
Looking
Is going up in a lift,
And wearing a mac
A mac-in-tosh
Is no more collecting sea shells
Is cinema on Sundays
And umbrellas
Is no more digging on the patches
Is train rides and baths

And is eating raspberries
And watching the trees
Is seeing them changing their colours and all the
    leaves is orange
And is no more seaweed all over your shoes
Is flicking a switch and is light
And is music sometimes, is saying Hmm I is wanting
    to listen to the music
And ding, is music
And is no more playing games with the children on
    the shore
Is working
And is walking on the pavement and is seeing crowds
And is a football match, and is all jostling crowds,
    and nobody is looking where they is walking and
    they is treading on my feet and is squashing and is
    shouting and always shouting
And is no more my father's old suit for weddings

Mill stops.

She starts again.

And is puddings
Is the Queen on the television
Wearing a hat
And I is seen the trees, and all the leaves is going orange
And is no more seaweed, is flicking a switch and is light
And music
And is saying I is wanting to listen to music, ding is
    music
And puddings and the Queen . . .
And football matches . . .
And puddings.

She wipes tears from her eyes.

And puddings.

SCENE TWO

Francis and Bill in the factory boiler room.

Francis

You can pretend there are windows.
You understand how these dials work?
Uncle Bill is you listening?

Bill comes over.

You must listen to me.
You are wanting the job, aren't you?
Lots of people here don't have jobs, you're the lucky
    one.
You just have to watch the pressure.
See here? If this drops below the red line, turn it.
Just a little. The marker should be staying between
    those two lines.
If it goes the other way, turn the handle. Just a degree
    or two.
It's all written down
Bill here, see is written on the side

Bill looks.

Bill

I's never had a job before
Only the patches.

Francis

Then the other thing is the temperature.
It's got to stay just at or around boiling.
Too cool and the machines stop working,
Too hot and the whole thing blows.
Okay?
Only it'll tell you if it goes wrong.
Is an alarm. Sounds like a bell.
You hear it, and you can adjust it again, by these levers.

Too low and you pull this one,
Too high and the other.
Is easy.
All you have to do is make sure it all stays constant.
See?

Bill is looking around the pipes.

Bill

Is nothing like the patches

Francis

Forget about the patches.
It doesn't help.
Forget all about the patches.

Pause.

It's a good job Uncle Bill. I've got you a good job.

Bill

Is a lot of pipes

Francis

You sure you's understood everything?

Bill

Is a lot of water

Francis

Yes. Boiling water
Tonnes and tonnes of boiling water

Bill

Where does it come from?

Francis

I don't know.

Bill

Must come from somewhere. Before it is boiling
Are we near a river here?

Francis

Who knows?

There is a loud noise above them. Bill jumps and covers his head.

    It does that sometimes.
    Its only an air lock
    It can make quite a din. You'll get used to it
    You may need to take your jumper off, it can get
    quite warm in here
    I'll have to leave you now.
    I've things to do.
    It is a good job, Uncle Bill
    You'll get used to it.
    You're lucky to have it.

Francis leaves.
Bill is alone. The pipes make a noise, he looks around.

SCENE THREE

Bill and Mill are sitting on deck chairs, in their garden.

Bill
    This is what H'England people do Mill

Mill
    I know

Bill
    We is from H'England now

Mill
    I know

Bill
    Is you happy?

He looks at her.

She takes his hand.

They carry on sitting.

An aeroplane flies overhead.

Pause.

Mill

We needs to see it

She looks into the sky.

We can't just be saying, okay is the end of it
We needs to be seeing it
Maybe we should be sending someone to see it
Then they come back and tell us
Is still our island isn't it?
Maybe there is some little part is okay
Just a little part
We needs to see it

Pause.

Bill is still watching the sky, Mill looks up too.

Bill

Second aeroplane today

They both watch it for a second.

Sometimes seems like the smoke is dividing the sky

Pause.

Mill

Maybe we could be sending some back to see it
Some of us
Just a few
If we all was saving and put our money in
We could all be doing that, couldn't we?
Someone be collecting it
And someone else be buying the tickets
Then they could come back be telling us what is like
Then maybe we would all stop being sick
Bill?

Bill
Maybe

Mill
What do you think?

Bill
I don't know

Mill
Some of the women been saying I should be the one
is organising it.

Bill gets up and goes over to the end of his garden.

*He becomes obsessed by the possibility of water all
around, although there is no physical source on stage.*

Bill
Where does that come from?

Mill
What?

Bill
There, this. All this . . .
Where does it come from?

*He picks up a patch of earth and squeezes it. The
moisture drips out.*

He turns to face her.

Are we near a river here?

Mill
I don't know

He puts the patch of earth back.

Bill looks either way along the garden.

Bill
I don't know either.

SCENE FOUR

Rebecca is standing inside Mr Hansen's office.

It is after the end of the working day and nobody is there.

She looks around anxiously

She knocks on the table once or twice in case someone is near.

No one appears, she looks around again.

Francis enters from a side door.

He is carrying a large bunch of keys and some files, etc.

Francis
Mr Hansen has gone already.
You'll have to come back and see him another day.

Rebecca
I isn't wanting to see Mr Hansen.

Pause.

Francis
Well no one else here, everyone's gone

Rebecca doesn't move.

I'll be locking up in a minute
Whatever you want will have to keep until tomorrow

Rebecca still shows no intention of moving.

Didn't you hear me?
You will have to go home.

Pause.

Rebecca
I is learning to read

Beat.

Yes, I is reading now

Francis
I'm busy, can't you see?

Rebecca
Can spell all sorts of things now

Francis
Good, excuse me

Rebecca
Can spell 'Francis'.

Francis
Excuse me, I have to do this

Rebecca
Sometimes I can spell 'Francis', sometimes 'Francis'
    isn't wanting to be spelt.

Francis
Go home Rebecca

Rebecca
I is only wanting to be talking to you
Nothing else, just is talking

Francis
There is nothing to talk about
Is there?
I don't remember there being anything to talk about

Pause.

Rebecca
Everybody been saying how different you is now.
Everyone been saying you is the man we won't
    recognise, is saying he looks like Francis but isn't
    Francis, if you were speaking to him you would
    never be knowing, is this person is working hard
    always always working hard, doing so well

Pause.

I is just wanting to be talking Francis
I is remembering when you were telling me about
    the piece of glass you kept in your pocket.
You still keeping that piece of glass in your pocket?

Beat.

That you was turning when you needed to be
    remembering how to change.

Francis
I don't remember.

Rebecca
Before

Francis
I don't remember

Rebecca
Is last time you left.

Francis
I don't remember.
I don't remember anything from before.
Nothing
Even you.
And it is 'I am' not 'I is', if you want to be talking at
    least be talking properly.

Pause.

Rebecca
You do remember me

Francis
You need to go now.
We both need to go. I have a lot to get on with

Rebecca
We were marked out from birth Francis

Francis

Look, you shouldn't be here.

The office is closed.

You can be coming back to see Mr Hansen another
time.

Please don't try to be talking to me.

Rebecca

I miss you.

Is all.

Francis stops.

He looks at her.

Francis?

Pause.

I is alone as you is here

Pause.

Francis

No.

If you're alone that's because that was what you
wanted.

Beat.

You wanted this.

Not me

All those months I wanted to talk

You wouldn't come near.

You wanted this

Rebecca

Please, Francis,

I wasn't knowing what I wanted.

Francis

It's too late

Anyway I'm not alone. Why should I be alone?

Don't think I am alone Rebecca
I am not alone
Out there is all of H'England.

SCENE FIVE

Bill is in the boiler room by himself, walking round the room and looking at the pipes.

There is the din of the air lock. Bill jumps.

SCENE SIX

Mill and Mr Hansen meet in a café.

Mr Hansen
Come in, I won't bite

Mill doesn't sit.

Mill
I thought you was very busy

Mr Hansen
Let me buy you a coffee

Mill
No

Mr Hansen
Sounds like you have been busy too

Mill shrugs.

How is it going?

Mill
Is just an idea

Mr Hansen
It's a good one

Pause.

It'll be hard work. A lot of money

Mill
Never been minding hard work.
Is got to see it, Mr Hansen.

Mr Hansen
Of course.
It's just,
It's very enterprising that is all. How much have you
got to raise then?

Mill shrugs.

Mill
Is enough.

Mr Hansen
How many will be going?

Mill
Six

Mr Hansen
Splendid

Mill
Is taking a camera, Mr Hansen

Mr Hansen
Good for you Mill.
Come on Mill, let me buy you a coffee.
Or a tea, maybe you'd prefer a tea?
I've got some news for you

Mill
Oh?

Mr Hansen
That is better
I want you to stop frowning.

You've got such a wonderful face if you stop frowning
I passed the message on about the houses
And the damp, it all went through

Mill

Oh.

Mr Hansen

They said it is in hand
They said they will consider it
They will consider it Mill, they want you to be happy

Mill says nothing.

When you stop frowning your whole face lights up,
    do you know that?

Mr Hansen laughs. He relaxes a little.

Prime sites
All over the city, if it goes through. New houses Mill,
    that is what we are talking
New houses Mill.
Built for you
Please sit down, Mill

Mill sits reluctantly.

Mr Hansen

So why aren't you pleased?
Isn't that what you wanted?
You said the houses were no good
Rain was coming through the floor

Mill

Why?

Mr Hansen

What do you mean why?

Mill

Why now?
We is been living in them already for is nearly a year

Mr Hansen

These things take time, they've come through now
that is the main thing.

Mill

What about the money for them?
They isn't coming free is they?

Mr Hansen

That will all be sorted, remember this is only a
proposal at this stage.
We'll sort that out later.
Let me explain. The front door, inside a hall. Maybe a
fitted carpet, maybe a lino floor, cork, who knows.
Further down, a living room. Open fire or maybe
central heating. To the end a fitted kitchen, and off
that a dining room – for dinner parties, whatever.
Upstairs bedroom one, the master, bedroom two,
for the children, and bedroom three a spare. Outside
garden to the back, along the side a double garage,
even a patio.

Mill

Where is all this money going to be coming from?

Mr Hansen

Have you ever seen a fitted kitchen Mill?

Pause.

So we want this to go through yes?
We want them to make the deal, there's some things
we can do to help
Mill don't look like that, you've got your worried
face on again.
Stop frowning
It's not going to be a problem
Okay? Keep smiling, it's not going to be a problem
If the deal goes through it is going to be a straight gift,
well nearly a gift they'll be some rent. Of course

there will need to be some rent
But it would be very knocked-down prices

Mill

We is not going to stop getting the six passages

Mr Hansen

Nobody is asking you to
Of course they are not
Nobody
You need to see the island one last time, or a picture
of the island, everyone can understand that, it's a
shame the navy didn't take photographs when they
went and then it would have saved you all this
trouble, but even still everyone can understand it.
I can understand it, but . . .
Postpone it
Take the houses. Settle in
Wait six months
Then send the men, and women
You'll get your pictures
It is to do with attitude, Mr Cavendish and his team
They want to know you are Britons
That you see yourself as Britons
You know what I am talking about
Start dressing a little like Britons
Even when you are by yourselves feel like Britons
At night
Even when you are undressed, that is the thing.
When you are naked.
Be Britons even under all the layers
It's good to be Briton, Mill
And the passages back to the island
It's part of the same thing
Just let the dust settle
Postpone it
It's just not good timing
Six men out of the community

It's not good timing

Mill gets up.

Will you think about it?
I'm working hard for you all Mill.

Mill
Is you ever doing magic any more Mr Hansen?

Mr Hansen
No

Mill
Is a pity
I was preferring you much more when you did magic

Mill starts to walk out.

Mr Hansen
What do you mean?
Don't just leave, Mill?
What do you mean?
Mill?

Mr Hansen in his frustration grabs Mill's arm a little too roughly.

He realises what he has done.

He lets her go.

Mill?

Mill leaves.

SCENE SEVEN

Mill sitting on one of the H'England chairs outside. She is working, counting money.

Rebecca is sitting on another of the chairs.

Mill
> You is always in trouble girl.

Rebecca
> Is never anyone wanting to talk to me
> That was why

Mill
> Be keeping an eye out for Francis.
> Can you see Francis?

Rebecca
> No.
> Wasn't wanting to be alone.
> I didn't know who they was.

Pause.

> Was a woman there
> That was only why
> They was the only people be talking to me
> She had a nice face
> I didn't know they had a camera
> Hair all shiny
> She was wanting to talk to me
> Didn't know she was from a paper
> Say let's be seeing you smiling, island girl.
> Let's be seeing you smile.

Pause.

> But then they is mean
> The woman was mean.
> They is laughing at me next.
> And they is asking all these questions, trying to
>   confuse me
> All these questions

Mill
> You shouldn't have hit her.

Rebecca
And I was telling her I didn't know the answers.
Is things I didn't know what she was talking about.

Mill
You shouldn't be talking to those people Rebecca

Rebecca
Then she said I must be simple was why I didn't know
Said all the islanders were simple.

Mill
Is said that?

Rebecca
Yes.
Said because we is all inbred too much.
Is never hit anyone before

Mill
Is said we is inbred?

Rebecca
Yes

Mill
How hard is you hit her?

Rebecca shrugs.

How hard?

Rebecca
Is very hard.

Mill laughs.

Is made my hand go all red.

Mill laughs louder.

So does Rebecca.

Mill sees Francis. She calls him over.

Mill
> Francis!

Rebecca
> Don't be calling him.
> Don't want him to be knowing.

Mill
> Needing a word is all.

Francis enters.

Francis
> Yes. What is it?

Mill
> Don't say it like that Francis
> Isn't an appointment system here.
> Is needing a word is all

Francis sits down.

> Be pouring Francis some H'England tea out of the
> H'England pot Rebecca.
> Gently.

Francis
> I haven't got long.

Mill
> Spend a minute Francis.

Rebecca pours some H'England tea.

> And using the H'England saucers Rebecca.
> Rebecca?

Rebecca reluctantly does so.

> I is had an idea

Francis
> Oh?

Mill
>Rebecca and giving Francis some H'England milk out
of the H'England jug.

Rebecca pours the milk. Francis and Rebecca are
awkward with each other.

>I is nearly raised the money now

Francis
>You know what I think

Mill
>Listen to me Francis

Francis
>Hasn't Mr Hansen talked to you?

Mill
>Rebecca be giving Francis a H'England biscuit out
of the H'England jar

Francis
>No

Mill
>Eat a biscuit Francis
Francis?

Rebecca passes Francis a biscuit.

Francis starts to eat it.

>I is nearly raised the money now
Is nearly got enough for the six to be going back.
Just to be looking.
And I is wanting to ask you would you be one of
them?

Pause.

>Think about it first
I know is a big thing to ask.
But I is too old, and Bill . . .

Francis

You know the answer.

Mill

Is as easy as that, is not thinking about it?

Pause.

I would like it to be being you.
I trusts you Francis

Beat.

Rebecca be giving Francis some more H'England tea,
And a bit of H'England sugar.

Francis

No Mill
NO
You know what I think
You aren't being sensible about this
What about the houses?
You need the houses badly.
Look at them. You should take the offer.
How else are you going to be affording them?

Mill

We need to be seeing it Francis

Francis

Why?
Can't you imagine what a buried island looks like?
Can't you surely?
A lump of rock.
So what?
It's a lump of rock now.
And who needs to see that?

Mill shakes her head.

Mill

I is sorry I asked you Francis

I is sorry I is wasted your time
Rebecca, Francis is finished his tea now.

Francis

I'm not saying you wasted my time.

Mill

Go on you don't want to go
Rebecca he is finished his biscuit.

Francis

It just makes no sense

Mill

Not to you

Francis

We just need to leave it behind now

Mill

Rebecca he is finished with his H'England cup now
Goodbye Francis, go and do what you have to do

Francis

They'll stop you anyway.
You know that?
You can't just walk in and buy six passages.
What, back to the island and you don't think they
    will realise?
They'll stop them
They said they don't want you to go back at the
    moment and they mean it
They will say the boat is full up or something,
I promise you
They are like that, you don't understand
They won't get back
It's the truth Mill, I'm only telling you the truth

Mill

Off you go

Francis
Don't be shutting me out, Mill

Mill
You is shutting yourself out, Francis

Francis
No
Is you that shut me out

Pause.

You and her
You are right I have finished my tea

He gives the tea cup back.

He leaves.

Mill and Rebecca look the way he went.

Rebecca
Has all of H'England now, is what he told me.

Pause. They both look the way he went.

Mill
We need someone who can be helping us.
If Francis won't then someone else.

Another aeroplane goes overhead.

They both look up.

Who is these people again?

Rebecca
Which people?

Mill
Your people. The people is from the paper
With the camera.
The one that you hit.

Rebecca
No

They is mean
They think we is simple

Mill

They won't be thinking that when they sees all the
    money we is raised
What is the name of the people?

Rebecca

You can't go to them

Mill

We is having to get these passages Rebecca
And if Francis won't help . . .

Rebecca

No

Mill

Maybe one of them could even be coming with us
Could be using their camera.

Rebecca

Is only one thing about us they are interested in.
I isn't thinking you will be wanting to be telling it
Not for no number of passages

Mill

What?

Rebecca

Is why I hate them
Is why I hit her.

Mill

Rebecca?

Rebecca

I is said I isn't knowing
Is only the old ones knowing

Mill

About what?

Rebecca
I shouldn't have been talking to her

Mill
Tell me
Rebecca?

Rebecca
Something on the island

Mill
What is on the island?

Rebecca
Something is happened on the island a long time ago
Something bad
Something bad even before I is bad
Is all I know
Something before the baptisms

Pause.

You know what I is meaning now?
Before Mr Lavarello is gone and come back with the
church.

Beat.

Mill
And they was asking you about it?

Rebecca
Yes
I isn't told them anything

Mill thinks about this.

Mill
We need to get those passages

Pause.

Rebecca
No, Mill.

Mill

We is needing those passages Rebecca.

We is never going to be able to live here until we is
   seen the island

Seen it buried

Seen just how buried

Seen it for certain sure.

Pause.

I'll have to be asking Bill.

SCENE EIGHT

Bill alone in the boiler room.

Mr Hansen enters.

Mr Hansen

Sorry, you're busy

I . . .

I'm not disturbing anything am I?

I don't mean to disturb you

I'm a good boss Bill

Don't think I don't care

I do care

Bill doesn't say anything so Mr Hansen continues.

It's funny, I own this whole place and it took me a
   while to find you

*Mr Hansen is rambling, he wanders around not sure
what to do.*

I heard you were the self-appointed chaplain on the
   island

I didn't know that

Maybe you, maybe you understand

What it is like to be the boss

All this and . . .
Do you think I have changed Bill?
I look at myself and I don't feel changed
But I . . .

He smiles, he's embarrassed.

Christ you were the chaplain . . .
The chaplain
I was surprised when I heard that
You?
Well I don't need to
But I haven't forgotten,
It's right up here in my . . .
Maybe that was when I changed
I should have said something
At the time, done something
After what I . . .
What you told me.
Why didn't I do anything?
What kind of man am I? I didn't say anything.
Didn't tell anyone.
Didn't say a bloody word.
What kind of man does that make me?
You answer me that?
What kind of man?

Pause.

I am a good employer Bill, I care about people
I'm a fair man Bill

Pause.

When you were chaplain
Did you have people come to see you, to tell you
    things?
I have a confession
A real one
Something I . . .

Well I need to get it off my chest
And I know you would understand
That is what they say isn't it? 'I need to get this off
    my chest, father'?
In the movies
Sorry, not father, I know
Just chaplain
Chap-lain
Like I said I have a confession
And if I tell you, maybe then . . .

Beat.

I lied
Bill did you hear me?
I lied
I lied to Mill
Of all people to Mill
Straight to her face
Not only that but . . .
I told you I needed to get it off my chest
I was paid to do it
Not paid exactly, not cash up front but
I got prettily heavily rewarded for it

Beat.

I told Mill that the island was destroyed
And I told Francis
And through them I told all of you
The island is . . .
Well it's not.
The lava only came to the foot of the mountain
Everything else is fine
The navy did go there and that is what they found
I've known for ages
Since you arrived practically
There are other reasons why they don't want you to
    go back

Oh and the best thing, the church
The lava came right up to the door of the church and
    stopped
Right there by the door
Even I would say that that was a miracle
Anyway there is no physical reason why you shouldn't
    all go back
Tomorrow
No earthly reason
Except, well . . .
The island is a pretty handy piece of land for
Did you see the war?
You heard of Hiroshima?
Nagasaki?
Well they . . .
They are developing them all the time
And a piece of land like that
No people
Miles from anywhere
Surrounded by sea
Secret
So Mr Cavendish
Well not just Mr Cavendish, but he is the man I deal
    with
Drew up a plan
Which involved jobs, houses
My bank balance
Defence is big money
A fake report
All the information that has circulated about
    volcanoes
Untrue, or at least untrue in your case
Your volcano turned out to be a sleepy little number
Fierce bark, but no bite
And now . . .
Hardly a smoulder

All I had to do was tell you all.
But you mustn't know this
You don't know any of this
You are in role as my confessor
What's the word?
Confidant
As I was yours
You can be silent
You can take this with you to the grave
We can both have sleepless nights
We can both see the people around us unhappy
You say a word, and I'll tell
Francis or the police or . . .
Who knows who.
The world if necessary.
About you.
The night before we left the island.

Pause.

Is that fair?
Don't think I don't care about you Bill
I do care about you, I care about all of you
Maybe even too much

Bill
Did you hold a gun?

Mr Hansen
What?

Bill
In the war?
You is said you is seen the war.

Beat.

Did you hold a gun?

Beat.

137

Mr Hansen
Yes
Did you?

SCENE NINE

Bill and Mill come outside.

Mill is leading Bill into the sunlight, he looks somewhat dazed.

Mill
Don't always be looking at the canal Bill,
Is a much better view this way
Come on, I'll set up the H'England chairs.

She sees the deckchairs are destroyed.

Oh

She tries to pick them up.

Is the wind
Must be the wind last night
The wind and the rain

Bill
Hold my hand

Mill holds Bill's hand.

Tears come into his eyes.

Mill
Is only the H'England chairs Bill
We can get some more
Don't cry
We'll get some more Bill, I'll get them

Bill stops crying, almost as if his sadness overwhelms the tears.

I'll get some chairs from the kitchen
We can still sit outside can't we? Like the H'England
    people do?

Bill stands there helpless.

Must have been the wind

Bill takes her hand again.

*Mill squeezes Bill's hand, then puts her hands back on
her lap.*

Is something important I need to tell you
Ask you.

Pause

I need to break a promise
I need to tell them about the time, before the baptisms

Pause.

Bill
Tell who?

Mill
The papers here
Is years ago I know,
Years and years
They is half knowing already, someone is told them
    something
I need the help of the papers to get the passages
We won't get the passages else,
Not them and the houses
And they will keep stopping them
They'll say the boat was full up
So Francis says
If we go to the papers, then they'll have to let us go
And we need to see the island

Bill can't speak.

Only they want to know something
Is what they want
Is like a swap

Pause.

I won't tell them everything
I won't tell them about you
Not if you don't want me to
It was all of us, anyway

Bill holds his head in his hands.

Bill
Can you hear pipes Mill?
I think I can hear pipes
Not just at work, all the time now
I is going to buy a map, Mill
See if we are near a river
Or maybe the sea . . .

Mill
Talk to me Bill

Pause.

Bill
All the time
Not just at work now

Mill
Talk to me?

Mill realises there is no possibility.

Just the basics, that's all I'll tell them

Bill
Was the worst, was the very worst

Mill
I know but then after you went away and is come

140

   back came the baptisms
You can't blame yourself Bill
It wasn't just you
Was all of us
We needed you to be the strong one
We might have all of died
You were, you were the strong one
Is no one ever blaming you
You did what you had to do
You did what was the right thing

Bill

All my life I is done the wrong thing

Mill

It was the right thing Bill
It was the right right thing
It was the right thing

Bill

And what about the baby?
Was that the right thing too?

SCENE TEN

Bill is alone in the boiler room.

He looks at the pipes and starts to turn the dials.

SCENE ELEVEN

Mill enters Mr Hansen's office.

Mr Hansen is looking out of the window. Silence.

She sits down.

Mr Hansen brings his attention to her.

Mill

I want you to write something down for me

Mr Hansen

I watched you out of the window Mill,

I could see you walking practically all the way from
your house to here

Your walk has changed, do you know that?

Mill

Will you take pen and paper, I need you to write
something down for me.

Mr Hansen

You stride now

Mill looks down at herself.

Then she looks back at Mr Hansen.

Mill

Take pen and paper

Mr Hansen

You even look different.

Your face

Did you have those lines before?

On your brow?

They aren't frown lines, they are new lines.

*Mill goes to his desk; she picks up a piece of paper and
a pen.*

She gives them to him.

Mill

Write

Mr Hansen

What shall I say?

Mill

I'll tell you

I've got their names here
Is the ones Rebecca hit

She gets out a folded scrap of newspaper.

Mr Hansen

I don't know why you are doing this
You don't have to have any more to do with them

Mill

Is the only way we are going to get the passages
You be writing, I'll be talking
Read their names for me

Mr Hansen takes the scrap of paper.

Mr Hansen

Cooper and Blanchard
Celia Blanchard. I've heard of her.
She's no good Mill

Mill

She is going to help us
Write
Dear . . . Miss Celia Blanchard and Mr Cooper
Sorry about your punch, start with that.
Then put, was a time before the baptisms
Have you got that?

Mr Hansen

Yes

Mill

Was the time that no boat came
And no boat came, and no boat came
And even after years and years, no boat was coming
Is all very well for people in H'England to be thinking
    we did a bad thing,
But there was no boat coming
No boat coming Mr Hansen.
They doesn't know what it is like when there is no

boat coming
Is you getting all this?

Mr Hansen nods.

And every day everyone has to be thinking this is
the day
And still no boat is coming
At first was okay because we had plenty of crawfish
But then the crawfish season was over
But we still had the potatoes
Then the potatoes was over
So we ate the pinnawins
Then the pinnawins were over
And still no boat was coming
You is still writing?

Mr Hansen
Don't tell them this Mill.
Whatever happened, it's your business

Mill
I want to tell them
What we is done we is done
I is not ashamed of what we is done.
I know all of H'England doesn't think much of our
little island
But I isn't ashamed of what we is done
The pinnawins were over, you is got that?
Then was the stormy season coming and we knew
that if we didn't have no boat before, there would
be no boat till after the storms had gone.
Certainly there would be no boat until for four months
Not even a chance
And we knew that we had to get through four months
And we looked at the food we is had left
And we is counted
And we is counted all the heads

And we is divided, so each person has a little bit of
　　food for all the months
But is no way
Is no way that the food we is got left is going to do
　　for all the heads for all the months until the end of
　　the stormy season
And even then we isn't certain that we is going to get
　　a boat
So we is all going to die
That is what we is thinking
Is you still writing?

Mr Hansen
　　Yes

Mill
　　Then someone had an idea
　　No point in everyone dying
　　I is never sure who said it first
　　But others is agreeing
　　Some of us can live
　　Is enough food for some of us to live
　　And so we is counted again
　　And we is worked out that the bigger proportion can
　　　　live
　　If the smaller proportion . . .
　　Seventeen people
　　People don't understand here what it is like when
　　　　there is no boat come
　　Don't understand what it is like to have no food
　　So was decided everyone put a button in a box and
　　　　draw out the buttons,
　　The first lot of buttons drawn out, they is the people
　　　　that live
　　The second lot, those seventeen . . .
　　They don't.
　　So was what we is done,
　　And then there is all this trouble about the buttons

everyone has to make sure that they have a button
   is like no one else's
Eventually we all has a button,
And we all put a button in the box
And each button be drawn out
One person is drawing them all out
And we is told if your button is drawn out is the end
   of it
Is no swapping
And we is all singing
Is a strange sort of singing we is done that day
I don't think is called singing really
And he is drawing the first few buttons
Then is drawn more and more
Mine is drawn, and Bill's is drawn
And everyone that is drawn out first is jumping for joy
Is weeping, just because they is okay
But those who isn't drawn
They just keeps on sitting there
Their faces is like stone
And they is not laughing
And eventually all the buttons that is going to be
   drawn is drawn
And those that is not drawn, is not drawn
My sister is there
Her eyes is so wide
But she is not crying
And that same day their food is re-divided
But the rest of us
We couldn't just watch them die
We couldn't just carry on with the rest of us living
Then someone else had an idea
Is the right idea, even though he is never forgiven
   himself
And he is got out the boat and he is told them to get
   in the boat

And all those people is got in the boat,
All seventeen
Some of them is so weak already he is had to carry
    them to the boat
And they is all sat there – rows and rows
Empty faces, old old faces
Is got so old all of a sudden
Even though my sister is younger than me, her face is
    all bone
And we is said goodbye on the shore
And then he is rowed them round to the other side of
    the island
Is cut off – can only get there by sea
Is a path, but is ugly
And he is rowed them there and is left them, with the
    little boat
And he is come back.
Is taken the ugly road through the mountain,
Is walked by the lake
And is come back without them

Pause.

And we is waited
And is the end of the stormy season
And there is a boat
Is a boat
And the boat is bring us food. Food and food
And we is asking why is we been forgotten?
Why is a boat not come for so long?
Why is no one brought us food?
And they told us there is a terrible war going on
All the world was at war
All the different countries is fighting
That is why they forgot to send a boat
They is been so busy
And Bill is gone back with them to see this war
And he came back with the church

And the baptisms
But the people is left on the other side of the island ...
Was long long dead
We was doing the right thing

Mr Hansen has stopped writing, he is listening instead.

Mr Hansen
Don't tell them this Mill

Mill
We need the passages

Mr Hansen
I'll get you the passages
Don't tell them this

Mill wipes the tears from her eyes.

Mill
When you live on the island you know what is like
when no boat comes

Pause.

You write that down, we isn't ashamed of what we
is done
We isn't ashamed.

Mill wipes her tears.

Mr Hansen sees her do this and gives her his handkerchief.

Mr Hansen
Don't tell this to the papers Mill

There is a loud noise outside the door.

Francis comes in, he is in a panic.

Francis
You'd better come

Mr Hansen
Why?

Francis
There has been an accident

Mr Hansen
Where?

Francis
Downstairs
In the boiler room

Mr Hansen
What?

Francis
Someone has locked themselves in
I think you had better both come
I think it might be Bill.

SCENE TWELVE

Bill, locked in the boiler room.

He turns all the dials at once.

The alarm sounds.

Bill
Is there a river near here?
IS THERE A RIVER NEAR HERE?
IS THERE A RIVER?

Boiling water spurts out from many different pipes at once and all over him.

It starts to fill the room, drowning him.

SCENE THIRTEEN

A few days later.

Mill is getting dressed.

She lays out the suit we saw in Act One.

She is in island clothes again.

Mill
Is no more puddings
Is no more anything sweet

Francis comes in. He is carrying a flower.

He tries to give it to Mill but she doesn't take it.

He puts it down.

Francis is still in H'England clothes.

Francis
Mr Hansen is outside

Mill takes the jacket.

Mill
Bill was wearing this the day he is married me. You
know that?
Is my father's before him
All the men is worn it, but Bill . . .
Bill is looking the best by far

Francis
He says he will wait all day

Mill
You be wearing it Francis, just today

She makes a move to touch it.

Francis
He let us all down Mill
Me as well
Mr Hansen let us all down.

Pause.

Mill
Was fitting him the best
Better even really than it was fitting my father and
    it was his suit.
Bill should be wearing it now
Tell them Bill should be wearing this
And when I is died I should be wearing the dress
I was wearing when we was wed
And even though we'll be in patches of earth on
    the other sides of the world, maybe it won't seem
    so far
Not so very very far
He was going to make old bones
Him and me and the patches.
Old bones.

Beat.

Stupid stupid man

She nearly breaks down.

She stops herself.

She looks at Francis.

I is nothing to say to Mr Hansen
Today is the day I is burying my Bill

Pause.

Maybe I should be putting this suit on top of his
    coffin?
Cover him like is a blanket

Mill picks up the flower and starts to put it in her lapel.

Go and tell Mr Hansen I is nothing to say to him

Francis
What did you tell him?

Mill looks at him.

Mill?

Mill
Is nothing

Francis
Must be something is made him change

Mill
Is something is gone now

Francis
Is about my mother?

Mill
Don't, Francis

Francis
Is about how my mother died

Mill carries on arranging her flower, but she is getting upset.

And the baptisms, I know it has something to do
with the baptisms

Mill
NO.

Francis
Why can you tell Mr Hansen but you can't tell me?

Mill
Francis.

She holds his head tight. She kisses him.

Today is the day I am burying my Bill.
Please?
Today is the day we are burying our Bill.
Francis.
Not today.

Francis
Anyway

You don't need to tell me,
I know already.
I've always known.

Francis kisses her. He is not being cruel, merely acknowledging the gulf between them now.

He starts to walks out.

Mill
He is loved you though

Quieter:

Always.
He is always loved all of us.

Francis has gone.

Mill is left alone.

She lies down inside the suit.

She throws an arm over herself .

She cries.

Someone knocks.

She stands up.

Mr Hansen walks in.

Mill wipes her face.

I was telling Francis to tell you I would be speaking
to you some other day

Mr Hansen
I never meant to lie to you Mill
I know I did
Of course I know I did
But I never meant to

She picks up the flower and starts arranging it in her lapel.

Mill
I is on my way to the church

Mr Hansen
I know

Mill
Today is the funeral of my Bill

Mr Hansen
I know

Pause.

So it's a certainty you'll go back then?

Mill
We is having a vote

Mr Hansen
It's a certainty

Mill
Some are saying they want to stay

Mr Hansen
But you will be going whatever?

Pause.

I'll probably never see you again. You know that?
Probably never see any of you
Those that go
Those that stay I expect I will be saddled with for a
     long time yet

Mill
I don't want some to be staying and some to be going

Pause.

If we is gone back straight away we would have all
     gone.

Mr Hansen

I'm sorry Mill
I am sorry
You could stay
There is still the offer of houses if you want to . . .
I know
Of course you don't

Pause.

I've got something to show you
Have you got my hankie still?
I can do it again
The magic has come back
All I need is my hankie

Mr Hansen realises this will get nowhere.

It wasn't my fault
Anyone would have done the same
What is it about that bloody place?
You, all of you
What the hell is it about all of you?
I let you under my skin
That is what it is
Like thousands of tiny pinpricks
So I did some business, so what?

Beat.

When I walked on that black sand something happened
to me.
That bloody black sand
What is it about it?
I've kept some you know, as a memento
I collected it while I was there

Mill

You shouldn't have been taking it

Mr Hansen

I wanted it

Mill
I wanted it
I wanted what you have
I wanted the whole thing
I even wanted you

Pause.

I don't have an excuse
I know I let you down
That was all I came to say really

Mill
Today is the day I am burying my Bill

Mr Hansen
I'll probably never see you again

Mill picks up the suit jacket, she shows him.

Mill
He wore it the day we was getting married

Mr Hansen
Will I?
I'll probably never see you again

Mr Hansen starts to leave.

Goodbye Mill

As Mr Hansen leaves, Mill shouts:

Mill
He was a good man Mr Hansen

Mr Hansen stops and turns.

Mr Hansen
There won't ever be a year without a boat Mill
Even if only one of you goes back
I'll make sure the ships keep coming
As long as I'm alive, I can promise you that.

SCENE FOURTEEN

By the docks.

Francis is standing by himself.

Rebecca comes up to him. She is wrapped up for the cold, and carrying bags.

Francis
Is everyone going?

Rebecca
Yes.

Francis
I thought they . . .

Rebecca
They's changed their minds
They is had another look at this H'england and
    isn't liked what they is seeing

Beat.

Francis
And you?

Rebecca
Me?
I is going because I is like nothing here.
And no one who can be living like that

Rebecca picks up her bags and moves on.

Francis
I didn't vote
I couldn't
I went in, I had the piece of paper in front of me
I saw the question.
'Do you want to return to the island?' and a big
YES and a big NO

And I couldn't do it
I couldn't decide.

Rebecca
I has to get to the boat

Pause.

Francis
Tell me what to do.
Rebecca?
Tell me what to do?

Rebecca gives him her attention properly for the first time.

Rebecca
Don't be asking me, Francis
I can't be answering for you
I is never been answering for you

Francis
Would you stay here with me?

Beat.

I could get another job.
Up North.
We could move up there together
Couldn't we?

Beat.

Have a whole new life together up there?

Rebecca
Is too long ago Francis
As you said, is too late
You and me
Is too long

Beat.

Francis
Or I could come with you

158

If you want
I could come back with you

Rebecca
No

Francis
Please Rebecca, tell me

Rebecca
No Francis

Francis
I want to hold you

Rebecca
Francis?

Francis
I is made a mistake
All of it is a mistake.
Please don't go

Rebecca
You'll be thinking about me until I'm over the horizon,
then you'll forget

Francis
No

Rebecca
I've got to go Francis

Francis
All you have to do is say and I will come with you
Get on the boat right now, go back together

Rebecca
No Francis
Stop this
You isn't wanting that
None of it
And I isn't wanting you if you isn't wanting that

It isn't me that you want
Not really
I know what it will be like, you'll be coming back for
    a bit maybe, is staying for while, and maybe things
    is nice but then in a few years a ship will be coming
    and you'll be going off again.

Francis
That's not true

Rebecca
Is true Francis
You could spend your life running between one and
    the other and not really living in either

Pause.

Choose
But be choosing for good
Look around you, is this what you is wanting?
Is it?
I is got to go

She starts to leave.

Francis
Rebecca?

Rebecca
I'll be waving

She comes back and kisses him, gently.

I'll be waving.
I'll be waving Francis.

MIDWINTER

Midwinter was first performed by the Royal Shakespeare Company in the Swan Theatre, Stratford-upon-Avon, on 5 October 2004, as part of the Company's 2004 New Work Festival. The cast was as follows:

Maud Ruth Gemmell
Leonard John Normington
Sirin Jean-Claude Thompson / Jonathan Magro
Trent Sean Hannaway
Grenville Pal Aron

Director Zinnie Harris
Designer Tom Piper
Lighting Designer Wayne Dowdeswell
Sound Tim Oliver
Music John Harris
Fights Terry King
Assistant Director Emma Stuart
Production Manager Simon Ash

Characters

Maud
a woman in her thirties

Leonard
an old man

Sirin
a boy of about eight

Trent
a pedlar

Grenville
a soldier, just returned from the war

A dead horse. A woman.

The woman drags the horse on to the centre of the stage.

She takes out a large sharpened stone and starts to hack at the horse's flesh.

She hears a noise.

She stands up.

Maud Who's there?

> *No answer.*
>
> *She returns to the horse.*
>
> *Another noise.*
>
> *She stands up again.*

Answer me.

> *She holds the sharpened stone out.*

I can see you.

> *She looks about in both directions.*

One move and you've had it. I'm armed. I'm a good shot.

> *An old man and a boy appear. The old man walks with a stick.*

Leonard We smelled the meat.

Maud Don't move.

> *Leonard takes a step forward.*

Leonard Couldn't smell anything else for miles. Half the city will be following us.

Maud It's mine.

Leonard sits down.

Leonard We know.

He signals for the child to sit down. The child sits.

Maud stares at them.

Well, eat it then.

Maud I found it.

Leonard We know.

Maud I dragged it halfway over the field. I risked my life for it.
It's mine.

She starts to eat. Ravenously.

Leonard stands up.

What are you doing?

Leonard Nothing.

She carries on eating.

Standing. Breathing. Looking at the moon.
(*To the child.*) Look. Look at the moon. No need for your alarm. I'm showing my grandson the moon.

Maud That isn't the moon.

Leonard Eat your meat.

Maud It isn't the moon, that's the sun, that is.

Leonard Of course it's the moon.

Maud It's the winter sun. It looks like the moon, but it tricks you.

*She speaks with her mouth full, the horse's blood
streaming down her chin.*

Leonard Whatever you say.

Maud The moon isn't red.

Leonard Neither is the sun.

Leonard lifts the boy up. They start to move off.

Maud Where are you going now?

Leonard Back. We smelled the meat. We came. We saw
you. We saw the half-moon half-sun. And now we are
going.

Maud I'm going to have to kill you, aren't I?

Leonard We don't mean you any harm.

Maud But think about it, you've seen the meat. My
meat. You could tell someone. You could tell the town.

Leonard They will smell it themselves.

Maud Don't leave.

Leonard The boy is starving. Can't you see that? Look
at his toes pinched into the ground. His hands, his arms.

Maud We're all starving.

Leonard You have a horse.

Beat.

Maud I had a child once. But then it grew. Not very big.
But big enough to give him a gun or a knife or a set of
arrows. Big enough to sink his nails into another man's
eyes. So they said. Don't leave.

She picks up the stone.

Stay where you are.

Leonard We can't. The smell of the meat will start to make us retch.

Maud How hungry do you have to be, do you think, to eat a whole animal? In one go? The head, the eyes, the belly, the penis?

Leonard It will make you sick. Once you start you won't be able to stop.

Maud So you don't want any then?

Beat.

Tell me you'd like some. Ask me for it. Take a risk.

Beat.

Boy.

Leonard He has a name.

Maud Boy, come here.

Leonard His name is Sirin.

Maud Come here, Sirin. You'd like some, wouldn't you? You'd like some of my sick-making flesh? To fill your tummy.

Leonard Don't.

Maud Why not?

Leonard He is starving, and you are playing a cruel game.

Maud laughs.

Maud He won't starve for long. They'll decide they need him soon.
 Then they'll feed him. Feed him up. Oh, there is food. Didn't you know that? We may be under siege but food does get in. After all, they need food to feed the ten-year-olds they call the men.

Leonard He's eight.

Maud So they'll let him starve for another two years yet.

Maud goes back to tearing great hunks off the meat.

The boy starts playing with pebbles on the ground.

Leonard remains standing on the other side of Maud.

She becomes self-conscious.

She tries to carry on eating.

The boy's game becomes louder.

Eventually:

Stop that. Tell him to stop that.

Leonard What?

Maud That. What he is doing.

Leonard It's a game.

Maud I don't like it.

Leonard He is a child.

Maud I don't like it.

Leonard signals to the child to stop playing.

Pause.

Maud tries to carry on eating.

Alright. Alright. He can have some. Not you. Him.
A small piece. I'll cut it. He wants it, doesn't he? He is
a good child, sitting there playing. Not grabbing. You've
taught him well. I like his manners. I'll give him a
mouthful.

Maud cuts a tiny slither of meat and takes it to the boy.

Leonard watches carefully.

She holds it in her hand.

Come on then. You want it, don't you? Come to me.

The boy comes and eats from her palm.

He's a nice boy.

The boy grabs Maud's hand and licks the blood from her palm violently.

He then starts to try and lick the blood from along her arms and neck.

Maud pushes him away.

Leonard Careful.

Maud He was going to eat me.

Leonard You have given him a taste. What is the point in a mouthful, when he needs a meal? He will return hungrier than before.

Maud You'll find a way. You'll find something. I know men like you. You'll end up giving him your own ankles to chew.

Leonard Sirin, stand up. This woman is harmless. We should go back.

Leonard helps the boy to stand.

Maud Look at his legs. He'll be dead within the week.

The old man and the boy start to move off.

Alright. He wants a meal. I'll give him the horse. The whole thing. He can eat it bit by bit. Over weeks. Or in one go. I'll give him the horse and he'll survive. But on one condition. You give *him* to me.

Beat.

My horse for your boy.

Leonard You're mad.

Maud It's a fair swap. I gain a child and he gains a life.

Leonard What do I gain?

Maud You lose. Your part of the gaining goes to him. Don't worry, I'll look after him. I'll take over where you left off. I'll show him the moon, sorry the sun. I'll do all those things. I'll do a better job than you did.

Leonard I did fine.

Maud But you didn't get him any meat.

Beat.

Leonard I need to think.

Maud Fine. Strut around a bit. Pull your beard. Anguish. Pretend you need to make a decision. There is no decision.

Leonard Who are you?

Maud Just a woman who has a horse.

Leonard goes to the boy.

He takes the pebbles from the boy and holds his hands. Gently.

Leonard Go on then. Eat it. The horse is yours.

The boy runs over to the horse and starts devouring.

What will you tell him?

Maud That you died.

Leonard He won't believe you.

Maud He'll forget you.

Leonard Yes, I suppose he will.

A noise in the bushes makes them both start.

Maud holds up the stone again.

Maud Who is there?

Leonard It'll be half the town. They'll have smelled it, I told you.
What a fool to swap a boy for a horse he must share with half the town.

Maud (*to the bushes*) Don't move. I'm armed.

Leonard It won't make a difference. They are starving. They'll storm you.

Maud I can see you. (*Looking all around.*) One move and you're . . .

Trent appears. He drops down on to the floor, his head protected by his hands.

He is carrying bundles.

Leonard It's a pedlar. Don't strike him. It's a pedlar.

Maud Stand up.

Trent takes his head from his arms.

Trent Two things.

Maud Stand up, I said.

Trent stands up.

Trent One: your horse is rotten, madam.

Maud Don't speak.

Trent And two: the war is over.

SCENE TWO

Maud and Sirin. They are inside a house, not a very comfortable house – maybe just a little bed at one end. It is evening, and Maud is trying to put Sirin to bed.

Maud takes a glass. Then she takes another glass.

Maud There is no milk just yet.
   I'm going to pour you a glass of water and pretend it is milk. Okay? It's a game.

She takes the jug and pours.

Here we go. We have to pretend these things these days. We'll have milk again before long, I should think.

She hands it out to him.

Do you like milk?

He drinks.

And then bed. You'll like it here before long. There is a garden out the back, and a river not so far away. You might fish there like all the little boys do.

He puts the glass back out.

She pours more water.

What do you say?

He drinks again.

Wouldn't you like to be able to say, more water please. Or milk, I should say, because it is milk that we are drinking after all. More milk?

He puts out his glass.

Couldn't you say that? You could even call me Mummy if you want.

She pours water again.

And then when I pour it, thank you. That is the polite thing. Thank you, Mummy, you could say.

He drinks it again.

And he puts it out a third time.

No. No more. You'll be wetting the bed, little one.

She takes the glass away.

He snatches it back.

You can't still be thirsty.

She puts her hand out for him to give the glass to her.

No, I said.

He doesn't give it back.

Sirin, let Mummy have it?

He drops it on the floor.

Pause.

We will say that was an accident. Okay? For today that was an accident, but if you do that again tomorrow, and the next day, it won't be an accident any more.

He picks up the jug.

Put it down, Sirin. I won't tell you again.

He drinks out of the jug.

Okay, so you have had your drink now, put it back down.

He drops it on the floor, where it smashes.

There is a terrible mess.

Pause.

What do you want me to say? Hmm?

   Do you want me to get angry with you? Do you want me to take you over my knee and thrash you?

   Pause.

Sirin, please clear away the mess you have caused.

   Pause.

Sirin. The dustpan is by the stove, please take it out and use it.

   Pause.

I won't ask you again.

   Pause.

   There is a stalemate going on between woman and child.

   Maud looks at the floor and makes herself busy with her hem.

   The boy looks at her.

   She pays him no attention.

   He goes to the sink and gets out the dustpan and brush.

   He gets down on his knees and sweeps.

And once you have done that you will use a cloth. There's water all over the floor.

   He carries on brushing in the same place.

You have done that now, please get out a cloth.

   He carries on brushing.

Sirin, you have got all the glass up.

   He brushes more and more furiously.

She comes over and takes the brush off him.

You have finished now.

She takes the dustpan away and empties it.

She brings back the cloth.

He uses it on the floor.

Thank you.

He hands her the cloth back.

She stands up.

And we won't mention it again.

She puts her arms around him.

He hugs her back.

Hey!

More and more tightly.

Hey, you are going to knock me over if you aren't careful. Sirin, not so hard. Sirin?

He pushes her into the table. She catches herself. He is still hugging her.

She manages to break free.

You have to be careful.

She sits down. He comes and puts his head on her lap.

She strokes his face.

Careful, okay?

She strokes his hair.

Careful.

He starts to go to sleep.

It is going to be harder looking after you than I thought.
I had forgotten what it is like to have a boy as rough as
you. The boy I had before was not a bit like you. That is
the funny thing, you were the same age but not at all the
same. He was tall whereas you are short, he was fat
where you are thin, he was clever where you are stupid,
he was good with words, where you don't have any, he
was always helping his mother, cleaning this and that,
whereas all you do is make a mess. But you breathe,
where he does not.

How dare you breathe when he does not.

She is still stroking his head.

Hmm?

She carries him to the bed.

She puts him in it.

Goodnight, my little one. We will learn to love each
other in time.

She covers him over.

Someone knocks at the door.

Shush.

More knocking.

The boy is sleeping.

*She touches the covers, then goes to look out of the
window.*

Go away.

Another knock.

I am not going to open my door to soldiers. Not tonight.
There is a boy in the house.

Grenville Open the door.

Maud I said no.

Grenville Mo, open the door.

Maud What did you call me?

Grenville Mo.

Maud That isn't my name.

Grenville Let me in.

Maud How did you know my name?

Grenville For goodness sake, woman.

She opens the door.

She sees him.

Pause.

I tried your door earlier, but you weren't here.

Pause.

Mo?

Pause.

Maud You are supposed to be dead.

Grenville No.

Maud I was told you died.

Grenville When?

Maud Years ago. Three years ago.

Grenville They made a mistake.

Maud I got a letter.

Grenville It can't have been me.

Maud They sent your watch back, and a few other bits and pieces.

Grenville My watch?

Maud I've kept it, I'll show you.

Grenville I am no ghost.

Maud You don't look like a ghost.

Grenville I'm not.

Pause.

She reaches out to touch him.

He takes her hand.

Maud But the watch –

Grenville They made a mistake.
Here is mine, still on my wrist.

She laughs, a sort of half-laugh, half-cry.

It keeps terrible time.

She hugs him.

She hangs on to him.

Maud I am not going to let you go.

Grenville I'm filthy.

Maud I don't care.

Grenville I spent ten years on a battlefield.

Maud Doesn't bother me.

He kisses her.

Grenville My breath stinks.

Maud It always did.

He kisses her again.

Grenville I am not well.

Maud No?

Grenville No. My lungs, they feel like –

Maud A few weeks' rest, you'll be right as rain.

Grenville Maybe.

She gets a chair.

Maud Sit down.

Grenville In a minute.

She makes him sit down.

She sits on his lap. She kisses him again.

Are you going to let me breathe?

Maud No.

She kisses him once more.

Grenville Ow.

Maud What?

Grenville You bit me.

Maud I want to eat you.

Grenville Mo . . .

He pushes her off.

She stands up.

Sorry, I . . .

He stands up.

Maud Are you here to stay?

Grenville Will you have me?

Maud Yes.

He looks around.

Grenville It's all changed.

Maud Not really.

Grenville Did you become domestic or something, this place it –

Maud It's exactly the same.

Grenville Less homely.

Maud The same.

He puts his bag down.

Grenville Who is in the bed?

Maud Isaac.

Grenville Oh
So this is . . .

Maud nods.

I never met him.

Grenville goes over and peers at him.

Sweet.

Maud He has your eyes.

Grenville Oh? My eyes.

He looks again.

Nice.

Maud They are shut.

Grenville But from the outside –

Maud laughs.

And the rest of him?

Maud You all over.

Grenville Oh.

Maud I want to eat him sometimes, too.

Pause.

Grenville I always imagined it was a girl.

Maud No.

Grenville Funny. I used to think about her.

Maud Him.

Grenville But in my head, her. Growing in your stomach and then, what she might have looked like the day she was born.

Maud Bloody.

Grenville But under the blood.

Maud Blue.

Grenville Then pink?

Maud Yes.

Grenville And the first time she laughed or smiled.

Maud He.

Grenville I know but –

Maud He smiled early.

Grenville Really?

Maud Clever.

Grenville Of course.

Maud And walked before his first birthday.

Grenville I'm pleased. And talked?

Pause.

Maud He doesn't talk much.

Grenville No?

Maud No.

Grenville Oh. Surprising after his mother.

Maud Maybe I talk too much, I talk for him.

Grenville Maybe.

Grenville looks over him again.

Do you think she will learn?

Maud He.

Grenville Do you think he will learn?

Maud I don't know.

Grenville He is still young.

Maud Maybe.

Grenville How old is he?

Maud Ten.

Grenville Ten?

Maud Ten.

Pause.

Why didn't you come back before?

Pause.

Grenville I tried.

Maud I don't believe you.

Grenville God knows I tried. I thought, if only I could get wounded.
I even danced in front of the bullets.

Maud You liked fighting?

Grenville No.

Maud You must have got used to the blood and the gore, you became good at it.

Grenville You never become good at it.

Maud Maybe you preferred it to here.

Grenville Never.

Maud Maybe it's too dull here.

Grenville This is my home.

Maud You are a soldier, you're used to different things now.

Grenville I love you, that is the same.

Maud You will kill us.

Grenville Don't be stupid.

Maud You'll get angry and –

Grenville No. Never.

Pause.

He goes into his pocket.

I got you something. Nothing really, I just thought, ten years I had better bring her something.

He hands her a package.

She opens it.

Maud A ring?

Grenville It was my mother's.

Maud I remember.

Grenville I took it with me for luck.

Maud But I'm wearing it already.

Maud holds out her hand.

It came, with your watch.

Grenville looks at her hand.

Grenville That is not mine.

Maud They said you carried it around your neck.

Grenville I did. I do, but . . .
Someone else's. Maybe all soldiers carry their mothers' rings.

Maud looks at her own hand.

Maud Maybe.

Grenville Take it off.

Maud It won't budge.

Grenville Take it off.

She tries.

He tries.

Maud Oww.

Grenville I want it off. You must wear mine.

Maud You're hurting me.

He pulls hard.

It won't move.

He pulls again.

She yells.

It comes off.

You're too rough.

Maud rubs her finger.

Grenville Now will you wear mine?

Maud You hurt me.

Grenville I'm sorry.

She picks up the new ring.

Maud What about the old one?

Grenville Chuck it out.

Maud But I've worn it for so long I'm fond of it.

Grenville It is someone else's.

He picks it up and puts it in the fire.

Maud It won't burn, it will still be there in the morning.

Grenville Then I will take it down to the river and chuck it in. We'll never see it again.

Maud Some poor soldier died.

Grenville Lots died. Don't think about them.

He takes her hand.

Put it on, Mo.

Maud No one calls me that any more.

Grenville Maud then, put it on, Maud.

She puts the ring on.

Thank you.

He kisses her hand.

You didn't want to, did you?

Maud Of course I want to.

Grenville I forced you.

Maud No.

He looks away.

What?

Grenville Maybe I shouldn't have come.

Maud Nonsense.

Pause.

Grenville I'm not well, Maud.

Maud You have a cough.

Grenville It's more than that.

Maud How do you know?

Grenville There is some parasite that lived off us, and carried something. Lots of the men have it. I feel like . . . sometimes I can't move at all.

Maud It's exhaustion.

Grenville Or my mind, it goes out of control, I scare myself.
My eyes water for no reason, that is the worst of it. All this stuff comes out of them, so much I can't see, and when I rub them it only gets worse.

Maud You haven't seen anyone?

Grenville Who would I see?

Maud A doctor.

Grenville Find me a doctor, I will see them.

Maud It's normal, I am sure it is normal.

Pause.

Grenville And if it isn't?

Pause.

I won't ask you to nurse me. That wasn't why I came back. If it is not normal, I'll go.

He takes her hand.

I love you. I always did.

Maud I know.

Grenville Now. You can eat me.

Maud moves towards him. He laughs.

SCENE THREE

The next morning.

The bed is rumpled. Maud is alone in the house. On the table in front of her are lots of pots of earth.

She is pouring seeds into each pot.

Maud We are going to have basil, and marjoram. And parsley. I am going to make fish pie and we are going to eat it with parsley.

She pours the seeds in.

She covers them over with earth.

And lemon grass. And thyme, and if this goes well then
I will dig up the back garden and grow rhubarb. The
boy can live off rhubarb and apples.
  Apple crumble.
  With rhubarb on the side.
  After the fish pie.
  Washed down with milk.
  From the cow I will buy with the proceeds of selling
my herbs.
  And my rhubarb.

  She gets out another pot.

And in this one –

  She picks up a seed packet and reads the side.

Cinnamon
  Cinnamon?
  Can we grow cinnamon in this country?

  She looks at the side of the packet again.

If they say so. The boy will have cinnamon with his
apples and his rhubarb.
  And his milk and his pie and his apples.
  And his lemon grass.
  And his marjoram.

  Leonard comes in.

Leonard The door wasn't shut.

  She puts the trowel down.

I said the door wasn't shut.

Maud I heard you.
  Why should I shut the door? I have nothing to hide.

Leonard Where is the child?

Maud With his father.

Leonard His father is dead.

Maud No, his father is not very well, but not dead.

Leonard His other father.

Maud His father and he have gone fishing, if you must know.

Leonard How can they be fishing, there's nowhere to fish?

Maud The river is open again.

Leonard Already?

Maud The war is over. Everything is getting back to normal, didn't you know?

Leonard It's winter.

Maud You can still fish in the winter.

Leonard comes in.

There is no need to come in. You can talk from the doorway.

Leonard You remind me of my daughter – have I told you that?

Maud pays no attention, carries on putting soil into the plant pots.

You and she, it is like you learnt language from the same phrasebook.

Pause.

I want to see him.

Maud You must think I am mad.

Leonard Just for an hour.

Maud No.

Leonard It is a simple request.

Maud We did a swap.

Leonard You tricked me.

Maud It was fair as fair.

Leonard Just an hour.

Maud Not an hour, not a minute. He belongs here now.

Leonard He is my grandson.

Maud Not any more.

Leonard He is all I have got.

Pause.

Maud Then have a pot of marjoram. In fact take some basil too. You can look after them, water them, talk to them, better than a grandson, really.

Or better still, a stick of cinnamon. See if you can make it grow.

She gives him the pots. He doesn't take them.

Leonard I won't go away.

Maud Take them.

She puts them down.

We are expecting a lot of the boy.

Leonard Sirin.

Maud I know his name. Only here he is Isaac. We are expecting a lot of Isaac. His whole world has turned upside down, suddenly he has a mother and a father, a garden that he can play in, a river that he can fish in, yesterday he had nothing.

Leonard He had me.

Maud He needs time to settle in.

Leonard I am only talking about an hour.

Maud Later. In a week or two, when he is settled here.

Leonard Now.

Pause.

Maud Close the door on your way out.

Leonard I am not leaving. Anyway, I thought you had nothing to hide.

Maud I don't.

Pause.

Leonard Does his new father know where he came from?

Maud What?

Leonard Does his new father know where he came from?

Maud Yes.

Leonard Liar.

Maud As it happens, I took the precaution of telling him.

Leonard I don't believe you.

Maud You know nothing about me.

Leonard Then you won't mind my mentioning it to him.

Maud I will deny it.

Leonard And the horse, you will deny you stole a horse too?

Maud Anything you say. I will get you certified. Locked up. You are just an old man, no one will believe your word against mine.

Pause.

His father isn't very well, I don't want you to come in and stir up trouble.

Leonard Why should I care about that?

Pause.

Maud Why are you so poisonous?

Leonard I am only asking for an hour.

Maud And I am only asking that you leave us be.

Leonard It is an hour, not a lifetime.

Pause. Maud picks up the trowel.

Maud I've got basil, and parsley, and marjoram. We are going to have a fish pie with parsley.

Leonard I don't want to say anything. You are a good parent to the boy, I can see that. Why would I want to jeopardise that? You have the rest of your life with him, you can surely spare me an hour?

Pause.

Maud Half.

Leonard Half?

Maud Half an hour. Don't ask me for more. It is half an hour or nothing. And don't thank me either, you didn't give me any choice.

Leonard Sirin and I . . .

Maud Isaac, his name is Isaac.

Leonard I will try to remember.

Maud That is the condition. Say it now – Isaac.

Leonard Isaac.

Maud Isaac, Isaac, Isaac.

Leonard I always hated the name.

Maud Never mind, say it again. Isaac.

Leonard I think I have got it.

Maud And keep reminding yourself, Isaac.

Leonard When shall I come?

Maud Next week sometime, I'll think about it and tell you.

Leonard Tomorrow.

Maud Impossible, his father will be here all day.

Leonard Not late afternoon, isn't he collecting a medal?

Maud You know more about us than us.

Leonard The town will be stopping for the ceremony.

Maud I forgot.

Leonard He will be gone a while.

Maud Alright, tomorrow, you can see him then.

Leonard I'll take him for a walk, or perhaps fishing.

Maud No, you will see him here.

Leonard With you standing over, poisoning his mind towards me.

Maud I won't interfere.

Leonard An hour alone with him.

Maud I'll do the washing. By the river. It takes half an hour.

Leonard I want to take him fishing.

Maud You must stay here with him. In this house. It is that or nothing.

Leonard You don't trust me.

Maud Not one bit.

He starts to go.

Leonard They won't grow, by the way. The soil is too sandy. Too thin, the water runs right through. You can't plant herbs here.

Maud It says on the packet –

Leonard They will say anything to sell you the seeds. Everyone knows that. You are so like my daughter in so many ways, but she would know that.

Maud Get out of here!

Leonard She would have known that from instinct.

Maud Get out!

Leonard It's strange. I thought all women knew that?

Maud Do I have to throw you out? Yell, and get the neighbours come running?

Pause.

Leonard It doesn't have to be like this, you and I want the same things.

Beat.

For the boy, I mean.

Beat.

Tomorrow then.

Maud In the evening.

Leonard I'll be here.

Maud Goodbye.

Leonard goes.

Maud looks at her plants.

She picks up a seed packet.

She tries to read it.

She throws it down.

SCENE FOUR

Grenville and Sirin by the river bank.

Sirin is sitting with a fishing rod. Grenville is adjusting it for him. He leans back in the sun.

Grenville The point isn't to catch fish anyway. That isn't why people come fishing. You'll understand that in time. They go fishing because it is what they do. Because it is a normal father-and-son thing to do, because they are seen to be normal if they do it. Because everyone thinks, ah yes, fathers and sons, that is what they do. Like kicking a football.

You never actually catch any fish. Or if you do, it's a bonus.

I've never seen a fish here, certainly not in winter, and I have practically lived in it for ten years. I've seen just about everything else. Things I wouldn't want you to see. Things I wouldn't ever want you to see.

It's funny, isn't it? Within days it just looks like a river again. But further upstream, where we were, you couldn't see the water for . . .

And on the other side, buildings. Already they are putting up new buildings. Isn't it funny how things change so quick?

He sits up.

Can you tell me something? I know you understand, but
I want to know why you don't speak?

You can talk to me, you know. Only you don't have
to. That is another father-and-son thing. We can
understand each other without anything having to
actually be said, if you want. Whatever you want.

Pause.

But the odd little word wouldn't go amiss.

There is tug on the line.

Now, what are you going to do? Isaac? You have got a
tug on the line, better do something or it will get away.

Isaac doesn't do much.

Wheel it in, like I showed you.

Isaac starts to.

You are going to have to go faster than that.

Isaac goes faster.

That is the way, faster faster. Have you got it?

The fishing line appears. Nothing on it.

Never mind. There is always next time. I told you, we
aren't here to catch fish anyway.

Isaac casts again.

You are good at that. How come you can do that
without being shown? I would say you are excellent at
that, I can't believe your mother has ever taught you. Do
that again for me.

Isaac gets the line out and casts it again.

Very good indeed. Has someone else been taking you
fishing?
Someone must have been taking you fishing.

Pause.

It's okay, I don't mind. After all, I wasn't around so I am glad that someone did.

Grenville leans back in the sun.

Someone may have started the process, but now I am here I will make sure you become a master.

Isaac continues to sit with the line.

SCENE FIVE

Outside the house. Maud is hanging out the washing.

Grenville and Isaac rush in. Grenville might be carrying Isaac. They are both excited.

Grenville Mo? Mo! Mo!

He swings him around.

Mo? Mo, come out here.

Maud appears.

Maud Don't call me that.

Grenville Come here.

Maud What is it?

Grenville puts him down.

Grenville Do it again.

Maud Do what?

Grenville He spoke.

Maud No.

Grenville Say it again, Isaac.

Pause.

Maud He can't talk, Grenville, I told you.

Grenville He spoke, I promise you, he said something to me.

Maud What?

Grenville I want him to say it. Isaac, say to your mother what you said to me.

Pause.

Isaac?

Maud You must have been imagining it.

Grenville No, now Isaac –

Maud Maybe it was a fluke.

Grenville I heard it.

He shakes him.

Maud Be gentle with him.

Grenville I am, I just –

Maud He's tired, perhaps he will talk later.

Grenville sits down with him.

Grenville He can speak, I know he can. Isaac? What is it? Why won't you say it now?

Maud He looks exhausted.

Grenville No.

Maud He's had a long day.

Grenville I have had a long day, I can still talk, can't I?

Maud He will talk later.

Maud takes him and hugs him.

Grenville You don't believe me?

Maud I didn't say that.

Grenville He will do it again.

Maud What did he say?

Pause.

Grenville He said fish.

Maud Fish?

Grenville We caught a fish, and he pointed to it straight away and said fish.

Maud You caught a fish?

Grenville It doesn't matter whether we caught a fish or not.

Maud I can make a pie.

Grenville The point isn't whether we caught a fish or not, the point is –

Maud I know the point.

Grenville I think maybe you are right, maybe you talk too much for him. From now on I think you should talk less around him.

Maud How can I do that?

Grenville We've got to listen to him.

Maud He will talk when he wants to talk.

Grenville But I think he wants to talk now.

Maud He is asleep now.

Grenville Later then. Before bed, we will try to get him to talk.

Maud Okay.

Grenville He said something else.

Maud Oh.

Grenville He said dada.

Maud Did he really?

Grenville I don't know why, we were just by the river.

Maud It is a universal first word.

Grenville I suppose it is.

Maud After mother.

Grenville He didn't say that.

Maud No.

Grenville coughs again.

Maud is concerned. She holds him while his body is racked with coughing.

Grenville Just the damp, we got damp sitting there.

Grenville takes his boots off.

I'll take him tomorrow.

Maud Where?

Grenville When I go to get my medals, I'll show him off.

Maud I would rather you didn't.

Grenville All the men, they would like to see.

Maud It might not be wise.

Grenville He is my son, isn't he?

Maud Of course he is, but the army – I don't want him to get any ideas.

Grenville What ideas? It's a state occasion.

Maud It isn't the place for a boy.

Grenville I want them to see him.

Maud I will bring him down later then, after the official stuff has been done. It will mean we don't have to stand around for as long.

Grenville You are sure you will come?

Maud Of course.

Pause.

Grenville You're right. Of course you are right. It would be too long a day for him anyway. It never crossed my mind. What would a boy want with a stuffy army ceremony? He would be bored out of his mind. You are so clever at these things.

Maud Thank you.

Grenville You don't need to thank me. It's you, you are the best the boy could want.

He leans back.

Who taught him to fish, by the way?

Beat.

He fishes well. You can't have taught him.

Maud Friends.

Grenville Friends.

Maud Friends' fathers.

Grenville I thought all the fathers were in the war.

Pause.

Anyway, it doesn't matter who. He can fish, that is good.
Every father wants a son who can fish.

Beat.

She strokes his hair.

Maud The two of you.

Grenville What?

Maud I love it.

Grenville Ow!

Maud What is it?

Grenville I . . .

Maud Don't look into the sun.

Grenville Just then I . . .

Maud It doesn't look bright, but it tricks you.

Grenville It comes and goes this, it just starts, one
minute I am okay, the next . . .

Grenville sits up.

It is like there is lemon juice in my eye.

Maud You should never look at the winter sun.

Grenville It's not that, they water for no reason.

Maud Open them for me.

Grenville It hasn't been like this for a while.

Maud You've been in the outside all day.

Grenville Sometimes I can't see at all.

Maud When?

Grenville Broad daylight.

Maud It's the time of year, I told you.

Grenville No. I think I am going blind. Or I think I know what it must be like to be going blind. I can't see and it –

Pause.

– it is all just black.

Pause.

There is nothing but black. And in the black . . . whatever it is that is in the black, it's –

Maud I know.

Grenville Just there, chasing my tail, just right there behind me. Catching up. Faster faster, getting there. And the only thing you can do is open your eyes and see that it is nothing. It has gone. Gone. Until you close your eyes again.

But if you can't open your eyes, if they stay closed, or you can open your eyes but you can't see . . . then what?

She strokes his hair.

Maud You're shaking.

Grenville I'm going to go blind, aren't I?

Maud I don't know.

Grenville I don't want to go blind, Maud. Anything but blind.

Maud We will get you some treatment, see a doctor.

Grenville There is an ointment, I heard there might be an ointment.

Maud There you are then, we will get you the ointment.

206

Grenville It's expensive.

Maud We will get it. We will sell everything that we have if we have to, we will get it. We won't stop until we have it.

She kisses the top of his head.

Grenville Kiss my eyes.

She kisses them.

Maud Is that better?

She kisses them again.

You won't go blind. Don't worry. You won't go blind. I won't let you.

SCENE SIX

Sirin and Leonard by the table.

The herbs are in front of them.

Leonard is speaking. Sirin is saying nothing.

Leonard P is for parsley. Which is this one. Look here, a P, in chalk on the table.

He walks back up to the beginning and starts again.

And L for lemon grass.

He does the same thing.

Can you see the L, Sirin? I am making it in the air. And M, of course, for marjoram.

Leonard is watching him.

I will teach you your letters. I always meant to, and since they haven't got you any toys, Sirin?

He sits down.

Why have you stopped, you say? You don't need to stop.
I have stopped because I have brought you something.
Oh Grandfather, what have you brought me, you say.

Leonard goes into his pocket.

He takes out a bag.

I brought you all I could afford.

Sirin takes the bag.

And you look in the bag, and you think, not bad, he
remembers that I have a sweet tooth, how could I forget
you have a sweet tooth, when I miss you as badly as
I do? All I can think about is your sweet tooth and
consequently I am running back and forwards to the
sweet shop all day long.

Sirin gives the bag back.

Aren't you going to eat them?

He offers them again.

Leonard puts them in Sirin's pocket.

Perhaps you will eat them later then. You can't have
grown out of your sweet tooth already? Hmm?

*Sirin takes them out of his pocket and puts them on
the table.*

Well, alright, I will eat them later then.
I still have a sweet tooth, as you know.

Leonard puts them into his pocket.

So what else have you been doing? That is what I say,
and you tell me you caught a fish. Well, I know that you
caught a fish because I saw you. And I say that I didn't
know that you could catch fish in the winter, and you say
that it was a special winter fish, and that you got to pull

its guts out and no doubt you ate it all for dinner with her blessed parsley pie this is how it goes on so on and so forth, backward and forward. Conversation.

I miss you.

I miss you, Sirin, terribly.

Pause.

Leonard looks back into the sweet bag.

I'm just eating this so I don't cry. You are not supposed to see your grandfather cry, though of course you have seen your grandfather cry all the time. And you are not called Isaac. Never. Always remember you were Sirin first.

He takes a sweet out and puts in his mouth.

Anyway, sweets make you rot. And which is better out of rotting or crying is a moot point.

He puts them in his pocket.

What would you like to do?

Pause.

And you say you don't mind and I say we've got half an hour, and you say it is less than that by now, and I say we could play a game, and you say we could fight, and I ask you if you like fighting and you say that your father is a soldier, and I tell you that your father is dead, and you say no, he is collecting his medals, and I tell you that you must never ever call that man your father again. Do you hear?

There is a noise outside the door.

They both look around.

Can't the infernal woman even give us the full thirty minutes?

Maud walks in.

I've only just arrived.

Maud Too bad.

Leonard You said half an hour.

Maud I've left the clothes to soak.

Leonard You must have done it quick.

Maud I'll have to go back and get them so say goodbye.

Leonard We have hardly had time to say hello.

Maud He doesn't speak, it doesn't take him long.

Leonard He may not speak to you but that doesn't mean he doesn't speak.

Maud He is retarded, he can't speak.

Leonard That isn't true.

Maud If he could he would talk to me.

Leonard Maybe he doesn't want to. Sirin, say parsley.

Maud His name is Isaac.

Leonard Isaac, say parsley.

Sirin says nothing.

Maud He is an imbecile.

Leonard Give him back, then.

Maud No.

Leonard You don't love him.

Maud That isn't true.

Leonard Not the way I do.

Maud More, I suspect.

Leonard You love him with some weird grief for another child, you don't love him for himself.

Maud Yesterday that might have been true, or the day
before, but now –

You know the funny thing is that if you had asked for
him back on the first day I might have been tempted. He
wet the bed, he smashed the jug, he bit me as I tried to
wash him. I thought, this is the worst child I have ever
seen. I thought about hurting him, really hard, hitting or
thumping him or anything just to relieve the frustration.
But then the next morning, seeing him sleeping, or
waking up and looking lost, or even the way he spooned
in his breakfast, and rubbed his eye . . .

Leonard Spare me.

Maud He snuggled into my breast as if he had grown
there.

Leonard How nice.

Maud You can't have him.

Leonard Then neither can you.

Maud Get out.

Leonard I need to see him again.

Maud No.

Leonard Every week, just one hour.

Maud I can't do that. You know I can't do that.

Leonard You will have to, you will have to find a way.

Maud I knew this would happen, I know men like you,
give you an inch and you will take a mile. I never should
have agreed to this.

Leonard You didn't have any choice.

Pause.

I have remembered why you remind me of my daughter.

Maud Not this again.

Leonard You used to play with her.

Maud I don't think so.

Leonard Katharine. You and her were friends. Your sister and you used to come and play with her. When you were putting out the plants that first day, I saw a mark above your elbow.

Maud I don't have time for this.

Leonard Little twins, used to be so hard to tell you apart.

Maud You have to be joking.

Leonard Magda had the mark, Maud didn't.
     Even Katharine couldn't tell you apart otherwise.

Maud You misremember.

Leonard No, because Maud died with my daughter. I remember pulling their bodies out of the water. And if you aren't Maud, you must be Magda.

Pause.

Maud Sirin, go and wait for your father.

He doesn't move.

Go and stand outside the door.

Sirin does nothing.

Move, I said.

Leonard Which must mean you are living in her shoes.

Sirin hangs on to her.

Maud Sirin?

She tries to carry him out.

212

He cries.

Leonard Tell me you aren't.
Tell me I am wrong.

Maud You are wrong.

Leonard I don't believe you.

Pause.

Grenville comes in.

He is in a good mood.

He takes his hat off.

Grenville Ah, we have company. I feel like celebrating.

He gets out a bottle of whisky from his pocket.

That is my last ever engagement from the army. That is
the last I ever have to see of the lot of them, and look –

He takes out a whole handful of medals.

– look, Maud, medals and medals. We can hang them
on the mantelpiece. You can play with them, Isaac, put
them in your treasure box. We can use them as buttons if
you like. Would someone please smile at me. This is a
celebration.

Maud Well done.

She kisses him.

Grenville A cold kiss?

She kisses him again, a little warmer.

Maud We have company.

Grenville I know, so why haven't we got him a glass
already? Have we met?

Maud He was just on his way out.

Grenville Well now he is on his way back in.

Maud He was going.

Grenville I insist he stays. Pleased to meet you . . .

Leonard Leonard.

Grenville A very good name. Maud, please, three glasses. Blow it, four, let's let Isaac have some whisky for a change.

Leonard I have been teaching the boy.

Grenville Good good, he needs to learn. What did you teach him?

Leonard His letters to begin with.

Grenville Don't tell me you taught him to fish. Maud, was this the man who taught him to fish?

Leonard Amongst other things.

Pause.

Grenville Well you did a good job.

Maud gets some glasses.

Grenville drinks.

Cheers.

They all drink.

So what else have you been teaching him?

Leonard The names of things, letters, things like that, how it is important not to mix one thing up for another.

Grenville Has he spoken to you?

Leonard Of course.

Grenville You see? You see, Maud, he spoke to him too. He doesn't speak to his mother, she thinks he can't.

Leonard He speaks very well.

Grenville Because he has an excellent teacher.

The boy holds out his glass again.

Grenville fills it up.

Maud No.

Grenville Why not, it isn't very often that his father gets decorated.

Grenville drinks his as well.

We will both drink, eh?

The boy drains it. So does Grenville.

A taste for it, eh?

He fills it again.

Leonard I don't think –

Grenville Just once in a while.

Leonard I know, but he is just a boy.

Grenville He likes the taste.

Maud Leave it, Grenville.

Grenville Half a glass as a concession to his teacher.

He carries on pouring.

A large half-glass.

Leonard He is just a child.

Grenville He is my boy, if he wants to drink he can.

The boy and Grenville drink again.

The boy puts his glass out again.

Leonard Sirin, no more.

Pause.

Put it down, Sirin.

Grenville looks at Leonard.

Grenville Sirin?

Maud His name is Isaac.

Grenville Why did he call him Sirin?

Leonard He shouldn't be drinking.

Grenville Why did you call him Sirin, when you know his name is Isaac?

Maud comes in between them.

Maud I have made some cordial, the boy can water his down with cordial.

She pours some.

Then we can all drink.

Grenville Will no one answer me?

Pause.

Maud He is an old man, he is confused.

Leonard I never felt younger.

Maud See he thinks he is young, well, clearly he is ancient.

Leonard My brain works as well as it ever did.

Maud More evidence of insanity.

Pause.

Leonard I would like a word alone with the soldier.

Pause.

Would that be alright?

Grenville You can talk here.

Leonard I would rather speak to you alone.

Grenville Maud?

Maud Don't listen to him.

Leonard Would you leave us?

Maud I don't want to go.

Grenville She doesn't want to go.

Leonard It would be better for her if she did.

Grenville But she doesn't want to, and I am not the sort of man to force a woman to do anything she doesn't want to do.

Pause.

Leonard Then another time.

Leonard stands up.

If she insists, I will speak to you another time. But I will speak to you. Thank you for the whisky. I am so glad about your medals.

Leonard goes round the table and kisses Sirin.

Grenville and Maud watch.

He leaves.

Maud takes a cloth and scrubs Sirin's face.

Grenville Where did he come from?

Maud I don't like him.

Grenville You have never mentioned him before.

Maud I didn't think it was important.

Grenville How do you know him?

Maud Not now.

Grenville Maud, answer me.

Maud Later. You put Isaac to bed. I have to go and collect the washing.

Maud picks up the washing basket.

Grenville Maud?

She leaves.

He rubs his eyes.

Maud?

Sirin gets up to leave as well. He knocks a chair over.

Isaac?

Sirin exits.

Grenville is left in the darkness of the blind.

Maud?

SCENE SEVEN

Late at night.

Maud by the river bank.

She wrings out the washing.

She looks out across the river.

She takes her shoes off and puts her feet in the water.

She sees something. She bends down to pick it up. She drags it out.

It is a soldier's hat.

She cleans it off.

There is a huge bullet-hole right through it.

She puts it back in the water.

She lets it float away.

SCENE EIGHT

The next morning. In the house.

Grenville is by the table. Maud comes in.

Maud I thought you'd be asleep.

Grenville No.

Pause.

I have been up for hours, I have been out already.

Maud Oh.

Grenville You didn't come back last night.

Maud I didn't want to wake you up.

Grenville I waited for you.

Maud You shouldn't have done.

Grenville You said you were just getting the washing.

Maud I got delayed.

Grenville By what?

Pause.

Maud The river, I was watching the river, I was looking for fish. I know that it is difficult to catch a fish in the winter but . . . you did, so I . . .

Grenville Bullshit. I feel like I don't know you any more.

Maud You have been away for ten years, it takes some time.

Grenville You aren't the same person.

Maud Of course not. Ten years, Grenville, I have changed, grown up for God's sake, had my thirtieth birthday.

Grenville It is not that.

Pause.

I had another attack last night. You weren't here. I needed you and you weren't here.

Pause.

Maud goes to the side and gets out a jar.

What is this?

Maud Ointment money.

She puts the jar in front of Grenville and puts the coins into it.

I found out about the ointment, and where you get it. When it is full, we'll be able to afford it.

Grenville How will we do that?

Maud The herbs are growing.

Grenville The soil is too barren.

Maud Maybe, but look. Little leaves coming. This one has a flower.
  And when they have grown, we will sell them, and then the ointment.

Grenville I saw the teacher. I just came back just now. I had breakfast with the teacher. He lives just a mile away. He says we should call the boy Sirin.

Pause.

And I am happy for that. I never liked the name Isaac anyway, if you must know. Sirin suits him better. Don't you think?

Maud It is up to you.

Grenville Your opinion is important.

Maud I prefer Isaac.

Pause.

Grenville Sirin it is.

Pause.

He said I should call you Magda. Not Maud, but Magda.

Beat.

Why would he say that?

Maud He is mad, I told you before.

Grenville No.
He seemed quite lucid to me. The things he told me, it seemed that I was going mad. Or you were mad, or perhaps both. He told me . . .

Pause.

He told me that Maud died. I am sorry I . . . And Isaac died with her.
Now why would he say that?

Maud How can I have died, I am right here?

Grenville He said –

Maud A mistake, Magda died, yes, I should know, I mourned her, but Maud, no . . .

Grenville The mark above your arm –

Maud We both had it.

Grenville Maud didn't. No, that is the thing, see . . .
     I remember she didn't. The night we first made love,
she showed me her arm with no mark on it, not a
blemish, and said this was the only difference between
the two. Maud didn't have it. That is the funny thing.
She didn't.

He sits down.

Pause.

So what should I do?

Pause.

We will call him Isaac if you prefer. Whatever you want.
Or Sirin, as I want. I don't care, but . . .

Pause.

I would rather you didn't wear my ring. That is the only
thing I will ask. Everything else, as you want. But my
ring . . .

Maud looks at her hand.

Take my ring off.

Pause.

It wasn't meant for you. It was meant for her.

Maud tries.

Here –

He pulls on her finger.

Am I hurting you?

He pulls again.

Why aren't you saying if I am hurting you?

The ring comes off. It has hurt her.

He goes to the fireplace and searches in the ashes.

Maud It isn't there.

Grenville Where is it?

Maud I threw it in the river as you asked.

Grenville Then you will wear no ring.

Maud As you want.

Grenville I want.

Grenville comes and sits back at the table.

They are building a new city across the river. Did you know that?
The first storey already.

Maud Oh.

Grenville You can see it from this bank. There are supposed to be jobs, Mo.

Maud Please don't call me that.

Grenville What did you say?

Maud Please don't call me that.

Pause.

Grenville I don't know what to call you.

Sirin comes in from upstairs.

Maud goes over to him. They embrace.

She picks him up and carries him to the table.

You don't have to lift him like that, he isn't a baby.

She puts him down.

He can walk, can't he?

223

Maud Of course he can.

Grenville Then let him walk.

Sirin walks.

Maud gets a chair for him.

You don't need to do that, he can get his own chair. Leave the chair, woman. Sirin, get your own chair –

Sirin pulls the chair out.

– and your own breakfast. You can get your own breakfast perfectly well. I don't like the way you have her running about after you. From now on you will do things for yourself a little more.

Maud He doesn't know where things are kept.

Grenville Then he can find out. Sirin, go to the cupboard and get out your own bowl.

Sirin doesn't move.

Stand up and go to the cupboard.

Sirin stands up.

Walk to the cupboard, and get out your own bowl.

Sirin opens the cupboard.

Maud He can't reach.

Grenville Then he will have to grow.

Maud reaches up for a bowl for him.

Put it back.

Maud He needs his breakfast.

Grenville He won't starve. He can learn to look after himself. I told you.

Maud puts it back.

If he can't reach the bowl he can eat off the table. Maud, pour him his porridge on the table.

Maud does nothing.

Pour his porridge on the table, I said.

Maud pours the porridge on the table.

Sirin sits down.

And now you can eat it.

Sirin eats it with his hands.

Not like that, with a spoon, you imbecile.

Grenville hits him.

Sirin cries.

Get yourself a spoon.

Sirin cries again.

A spoon, I said.

He hits him again.

He doesn't even know where the spoons are kept. Maud, what have you been teaching this child? Well if he doesn't know where the spoons are, there is no point in his having breakfast. No breakfast today, Isaac. Go and clean yourself up.

Sirin looks at him.

He hits him again. Hard.

Go and clean yourself up.

Sirin goes to the sink.

Leave him, Maud, he has to learn.

Maud makes a move towards Sirin, Grenville grabs her arm and stops her.

You mustn't be soft on him.

Sirin is snivelling.

Grenville pushes him. Hard.

Clean up, I said.

Sirin does nothing. Another push. Sirin falls to the floor.

Clean up. Can't you hear me?

Grenville kicks the child, who curls up on the floor. Once, twice. Three times.

Sirin cries out. Maud tries to intervene again, but Grenville grabs her and pushes her, roughly.

I won't have you being soft on him either.

Grenville stands up.

I have to go into town. I don't know how long I will be.
The teacher is coming this morning for his lesson as always. I said you would be here and would welcome him. No arguments, it is good for the boy to learn. There are lots of things this boy has to learn. And if he doesn't learn you will have to learn to beat him too. Hard, until he breaks. We will both have to learn to beat him.

Grenville walks out.

Maud picks up Sirin and comforts him.

Maud Shush shush, there you go. You are okay now. Hey little one, you are okay.

She rocks him.

I'll make you some breakfast. He has gone now. It's okay, my love.

SCENE NINE

Leonard is outside his house. He is planting some shrubs.
Maud and Sirin arrive.
She is carrying Sirin on her hip.
She watches him.

Maud So he hit you too.

   Leonard turns round.

Leonard Just a bruise, nothing.

Maud It looks more than that.

Leonard I was just coming to you.

Maud Why did you tell him?

Leonard He threatened me.

Maud We could have kept it going, but now . . .

Leonard You weren't going to let me see the boy, were you?

   Sirin cries.

Maud It's okay.

Leonard What has happened to him?

Maud He is okay.

Leonard He is frightened.

Maud He will be alright. His father has a temper, you know that.

   Maud puts him down.
   Sirin hangs on to her.

Go to your grandfather.

Sirin won't move.

It is your grandfather, go to him.

Leonard Here, Sirin?

Sirin hangs on to her.

Maud You will have to take him.

Leonard I thought you wanted him.

Maud I can't keep him, not now.

Leonard You mean he should come here?

Maud Grenville has turned back into a soldier. He will kill him before long, this morning I saw it, just a little hit but now he knows he isn't his . . .

Leonard I can't take him.

Maud He is your grandchild.

Leonard But you said yourself, I am getting old. You know I can't.

Maud You said you wanted him.

Leonard When you had him, I wanted him, but now –

Maud Grenville will kill him.

Leonard You will have to find somewhere else for him.

Maud He is your grandchild.

Leonard It doesn't count for anything.

Pause.

I can't manage, and anyway, for how long? I am finding it more and more difficult to look after myself, but with a child.

Maud What about for your daughter's sake?

Leonard Katharine.

Maud Katharine.

Leonard Don't say it as if you don't know her name.

Maud What about for Katharine?

Leonard She didn't love him any more than I did. She was always wishing him on someone else. She tried to lose him when she was pregnant, she twisted her ankle trying to abort, and when he was born he was such a strange child, it was the same. The silence, it drives you mad. You have to have both sides of the conversation to yourself. No one can live with that.

Maud He will learn.

Leonard He won't learn. He is eight already. He should have learnt by now.

Maud He said fish.

Leonard No.

Maud Grenville said he said fish.

Leonard You didn't even hear it yourself? The number of times I have thought I heard him say something, one word maybe in amongst the silence, but even if he did, what is one word when he needs a dictionary to be able to talk? Conversation, Maud, is made of more than one word. Fish, he says, oh, you say, fish, he says again, ah, you say, fish from him a third time, it doesn't add up to much, does it? He is an imbecile, face it.

Pause.

A little bruising from his father won't harm him. Like it won't harm me. You can continue to bring him here for his lessons, if you need a break. Once a week for an hour or so. I would like that.

Maud I can't live that way.

Leonard Then you will have to find another way by yourself.

Maud looks at his plants.

Maud How come your plants do so well? The soil is the same, and yet yours are twice the size.

Leonard I add chalk. The soil is too full of sand. It doesn't hold the water, the plants dry out. So I add a little chalk.

Maud nods.

Maud Where do you get the chalk from?

Leonard It is dangerous. Lime, you have to dig it with your hands.

Maud Could you get me some?

Leonard You have to be careful, if you add it to water it corrodes. Skin, flesh, bone, whatever comes in its path. I knew a man who dropped a little on his hand, then with the rain, a hole straight through.

Maud The marjoram would benefit, you say.

Leonard Just a little, under the surface. To counteract the sand.

Maud Would you get me some? I think the herbs could do with some.

Leonard Of course.

Pause.

You will learn the way of the plants. You are clever, you will soon get the hang of it.

And the boy, you will soon learn the way of him. Even the father. You'll soon get the way. Plenty have before you. You'll manage.

SCENE TEN

Grenville by the river.

He takes his boots off.

He gets out his fishing line.

He can't see any more.

Grenville Just because I can't see you, doesn't mean
I won't catch you.

 He rubs his eyes.

Just because I . . . I can sense that you are there. And
I am right behind you. I am on your tail. I will get you,
little fishes, don't worry.

 He rubs his eyes again.

No, not here.

 He rubs them again.

Stop. Stop, I said, I know you aren't there. There is
nothing there, you black. STOP, STOP.

 The pedlar comes and sits down next to him.

Who is that?

 Grenville turns round.

Trent Your line isn't out.

Grenville I know.

Trent You won't catch anything that way.

Grenville I can see.

Trent I just thought you might like . . .

Grenville No thank you.

Grenville re-casts.

Trent You've all got it, haven't you?

Pause.

This parasite. A whole generation of blind soldiers.

Grenville I am not blind.

Trent Not yet.

Trent looks across the river to the other side.

That is going to be one of my houses over there. I don't know if you can see it, but one of the new ones. First storey going up already. You see the staircase. Just up to the landing. Got my name down and everything.

It's a good job that all you soldiers have gone blind, because, whatever happens, the war can't start again, can it?

He chuckles.

The war can't start because who the hell would they fight with?

Grenville grabs him and holds his throat.

Get off.

Grenville Who are you anyway?

Trent Just a pedlar.

Grenville I am not going blind.

Trent I didn't say.

Grenville I am not going blind.

Trent Listen, mister, you are hurting me.

Grenville throttles him more.

Eventually he stops.

The pedlar draws breath, obviously really hurt by it.

He gets up.

Grenville is sitting up.

The pedlar kicks him. Once, twice.

Grenville does nothing.

The pedlar leaves.

Grenville cries.

SCENE ELEVEN

Back at the house.

Maud has laid the table. There is a cloth, and on it flowers.

She has laid the table for two.

She might even light a candle.

Grenville comes in.

He opens the door.

He has a little difficulty walking to the table.

Maud notices and takes his hand. She leads him to the table.

She pulls out a chair.

Grenville Thanks.

She kisses the top of his head.

I tried to catch a fish.

Maud It is very hard to catch a fish in winter.

Pause.

She puts a plate of food down in front of him.

Grenville What is it?

Maud Vegetables.

Grenville Oh.

Maud Parsnips and carrots.

Grenville Where is Isaac?

Maud Asleep. I put him to bed early.

Grenville I am going to teach him to talk. I decided.

Maud Of course.

Grenville If others can talk then so can he.

Pause.

Grenville looks down at the plate.

I can't see it, Maud. Carrots and parsnips. That should be orange and white, shouldn't it, all I see is grey.

Maud The light isn't very good.

Grenville It isn't the light, and after the grey comes black.

Pause.

Maud I got you something today.

Grenville Oh.

Maud Some ointment. I've made it up already.

Grenville Where did you get it from?

Maud I sold all the plants. The apples from the back. I sold just about everything that we had.

Grenville Did you see a doctor?

Maud Of course.

She gets out a little plate of white stuff.

He said you will be right as rain.

She takes it over to him.

He said it will soothe the eyes, get rid of the infection. It can all be reversed.

Grenville Let me feel.

He puts his fingers into it.

Maud Doesn't that feel nice?

Grenville What did the doctor look like?

Maud Old and kindly. He said it was the same with all the soldiers.

Grenville His voice?

Maud Soothing. He had seen it all before.

Grenville Was he a good doctor?

Maud Of course he was.

Grenville Put it on for me.

She stands behind him.

She puts it on with her fingers.

Maud There we are. How does it feel?

Grenville Cold.

Maud Don't shut them, keep them open if you can.

Grenville Will it sting?

Maud Only a little.

She carries on putting it on him.

I may be Magda, Grenville, and not Maud, but it doesn't mean that I don't love you. I always loved you, you know that. Even when I was a kid I loved you, and then when we were teenagers, and all you could see was Maud, I was still loving you. Fiercer even. The more you and she became inseparable the more I wanted . . . Standing on the sidelines trying to say, love Magda, love Magda. But it was always Maud. Maud Maud Maud.

Grenville Don't . . .

Maud I wish I had been Maud, Grenville. That is all. My whole life I wish I had been Maud. And if I could be, I would.

Pause.

How does it feel now?

Grenville Hot.

Maud That is all. We've nearly finished it now.

Grenville It isn't ointment, is it?

Pause.

It is stinging, Maud. You must feel that on your fingers. The tears in my eyes, they are making it worse. What are you waiting for? If it is lime, it needs water. Simple chemistry tells you that. If it is to eat through my skull you must add water. There is water on the table, I am sure you took the precaution of that. Throw a glass of water in my face, Maud, and it will be over.

Maud picks up the glass.

Don't hesitate now. What? At the final hurdle, you hesitate? Maud wouldn't have. If she had planned to do something she . . .

Maud throws the glass of water in his face.

The water reacts with the lime. Steam comes off.

Grenville screams.

She holds him while he screams.

Maud It's okay, it's okay.
Shush. It is okay.

SCENE TWELVE

Trent sitting by the river bank.

*He takes his boots off. He looks over to the other bank.
He sees something.*

Trent Oi. Why is there no one working today? It's not
a Sunday. Where has everyone gone? You've only got
halfway up to the first landing. I need a second storey
on my house if I am to live there. Hey?
Where is everyone? Why has the work stopped?

*He picks up a stone and throws it over to the other
bank.*

Is there no one there?
What about my house?

He picks up another stone and throws it.

What about my house? You can't just stop now?

SCENE THIRTEEN

Maud and Sirin outside.

They are playing on a rug.

Sirin Fish.

Maud Fish and fish and fish, my love.

Sirin Fish fish fish fish.

Maud You say it loud.

Sirin Fish.

Maud laughs.

Fish.

She laughs again.

Maud Who said you can't have a conversation with a single word?

Sirin Fish fish fish.

Leonard comes in.

Maud Look, we are talking. He says fish and then I say fish and then he says fish and on and on, until we have discussed the cares of the world and philosophy and told each other long rambling stories about epic tales and laughed at complex and subtle jokes. You wouldn't believe the jokes he can tell. The punchlines he can dream up with a single word. Tell your jokes now, Sirin. Well, he is shy now, but the jokes . . .

Leonard sits down.

You would laugh at the jokes, I know you would.

Leonard Your plants?

Maud Flourishing.

Leonard It did the trick?

Maud You knew it would.
You?

Leonard All healed.

Maud Good.

Pause.

The best one is this one he tells about this man who –

Leonard I have just come from the town.

Pause.

Maud Anyway the man, he doesn't know whether he –

Leonard The war is starting again.

Pause.

That is what they are saying.

Maud It's a joke.

Leonard No joke.

Maud A rumour then, the war is over.

Leonard I thought it was a rumour, so I went up to a town official and asked him, is it a rumour, I asked.

Maud He said of course it is.

Leonard He said he wished it were. There were tears in his eyes. It's a new war, he said.

Pause.

You talk about jokes, well, he told me one. And he wasn't a funny man. But this one, a funny thing. How can it be? I said to him, this new war, how can we go to war? What do you mean, he said to me, we can go to war as easily as we can clap our hands. It wasn't the answer I expected so I went on. But the soldiers, I said. What about the soldiers, he said. The soldiers are all sick, they have this parasite. The soldiers, he asked. Yes, the soldiers, I said.

And do you know what he said to me then?

This next war won't need soldiers.

Pause.

That is the punchline, by the way. This next war won't need soldiers. I laughed at that, he was serious. How can there be a war without soldiers? I said. He didn't answer.

Pause.

It's impossible, isn't it? Like a self-defeating . . .
HOW CAN THERE BE A WAR WITHOUT SOLDIERS? I said.

Pause.

Maud We have been sitting in the sun, and . . .

Leonard How can there be?

Pause.

Maud In this house, whatever happens out there, in this house . . .

Leonard Maud?

Maud Peacetime. That is all I know.

Pause.

It's peacetime here, you understand. There is no more of this, not here. Not just as Sirin is learning to talk. No, not now. We are in a different land to out there. They're in one season, but we are in another. You understand? In the four walls of the garden –

Leonard I don't even understand it.

Maud So don't mention it. It's gone. You didn't go into the town today, you won't again. They might have rumours over there, they might not. It doesn't affect us, does it? What we are is what we are here. That's all. Nothing more. Three souls and a house.
And a sky and a sun.
A garden.

The plants will grow or not. Sirin will talk or not. We will eat or not. That is it. It's over, do you understand me? There is no war.

Leonard Even as . . .?

Maud Peacetime.

Leonard looks at the sky.

Leonard The sun.

Maud And the four walls of the house. That's all.

Leonard Peacetime then.

Sirin claps.

Maud claps back.

Maud Peacetime.

HOW TO HOLD YOUR BREATH

for my sister

Thanks to the following:

Nikki Amuka-Bird, Pippa Bennett-Warner,
Adam Best, Vera Chok, Darrell D'Silva,
Sam Troughton, Debbie Hannan, John Harris,
Mark and Fran Shaw, Frances Poet,
Dinah Wood, Steve King and Mel Kenyon.

Above all, thanks to Vicky Featherstone –
collaborator, encourager, inspiration and friend.

How to Hold Your Breath was first performed at the Royal Court Jerwood Theatre Downstairs, London, on 4 February 2015. The cast was as follows:

Dana Maxine Peake
Jarron Michael Shaeffer
Jasmine Christine Bottomley
Interviewer / Doctor / Clara Danusia Samal
Interviewer / Marta / Telephone Operator
    Siobhán McSweeney
Interviewer / Train Inspector / Punter Neil D'Souza
Librarian Peter Forbes
Ensemble Joshua Campbell, Raghad Chaar,
    Soledad Delahoz, Marisa Flamino, Michael Jinks,
    Djordje Jovanovic, Connor Mills, Mark Ota,
    Aaron Peters, Alison Porter, Ruth Pugh, Javier Rasero,
    Jessica Simet, Ben Tiramani, Temi Wilkey

Director Vicky Featherstone
Designer Chloe Lamford
Lighting Designer Paule Constable
Composer Stuart Earl
Sound Designer Gareth Fry
Movement Director Ann Yee
Assistant Director Debbie Hannan

Characters

Dana
a woman in her late twenties

Jarron
a man who works for the UN

Jasmine
Dana's sister

Librarian
a book worm

Train Inspector

Woman
telephone operator

Punter
a man looking for sex

Marta
a woman who used to be on TV

Clara
a woman who used to be a lawyer

Doctor

The Interview Panel
three voices

Note on Punctuation

The spoken lines in this text start with a lower-case letter to stop each line reading like a statement; lines are often incomplete phrases, half-thoughts or utterances that pass from one to another, and are rarely whole sentences.

In general the spoken text is laid out according to each character's process of reasoning with each new line indicating a new thought.

ONE

Dana speaks to the audience.

Dana
I am stand at the back. Don't look out. Gets shouted
at for looking down. I am eyes closed, head bent in
every gathering. I am knees bowed, chest to the floor.
I am a flower by the wall, grass in the shade. I am
back turned, shoulders hunched, face hollowed. I am
a scream. A howl. I am a snake on the plane, a hyena,
an antelope. I am ant under a stone, beetle scurrying
away. I am beaten at birth, blackened. I am sand. I am
soil. I am earth. I am less than earth. I am poor. I'm so
poor my skin is my clothes. I am uncovered. Ashamed.
The land can't feed me. I am the end. The dead. The
carcass by the roadside. I am the abyss into which
people dread to fall.

She stops and looks at herself in the mirror.

She takes a deep breath.

TWO

Europe.

*In a cosy room two lovers lie under the covers
intertwined and heavy with sleep. The woman, Dana, is
in her late twenties. The man, Jarron, is a little older.*

Dana sits up.

Jarron
don't do that

Dana
I had such a strange dream

Jarron
it's not even morning yet

Dana
but the sun's up

Beat.

hey the sun's up

Jarron
so the sun's up, we can sleep a bit longer, can't we?

Dana
we could

Jarron
then why don't we?

He pulls her back down.

She laughs.

He covers her with the sheet.

She lets him.

He kisses her.

She kisses him back.

Dana
you've got a scar on your chest

Jarron
that was where they ripped my soul out.

Dana
very funny.

They kiss again.

He rolls on top of her.

Dana
actually I'm quite hungry

Jarron
what?

Dana
aren't you?
I mean don't you want something to eat?

Jarron
not particularly

Dana
don't you eat where you come from?

Jarron
sometimes but not in the middle of –

Dana
have some fruit then, some bread
it's breakfast time

Jarron
seriously?

Dana
seriously
I'm starving.

Jarron
alright. What do you have?

Dana
what do you want?

Jarron
what have you got?

Dana
there's a shop downstairs
anything you can imagine

Jarron
  they're open at this time?

Dana
  it's not early. It's getting late

Jarron
  surprise me

Dana
  croissants, coffee, juice, cake

Jarron
  sounds delicious

He grabs her.

She squeals.

They kiss for a moment.

again

They kiss some more.

Dana
  you're greedy

Jarron
  of course

Dana
  you'd think you'd never been kissed –

Jarron
  not by you

Dana
  you have to be quiet, I share this flat

Jarron
  I don't care

Dana
  actually, seriously

Jarron
  you're quite hungry

Dana
  finally he hears!

Jarron
  you think I've had my time

Dana
  shut up

Jarron
  you're bored and want to get rid of me

Dana
  never

Jarron
  that's why you looked at the sun

Dana
  the day has begun, that's all

Jarron
  I'll pay you extra

Dana
  what?

Jarron
  I'll give you a bit more

Dana
  a bit more what?

Jarron
  money
  you're a business woman, I know how this works

Dana
you think you are paying?

Jarron
aren't I?

Dana
what?

Jarron
what?

Dana
what?

Jarron
now wait a minute –

Dana
fucking cheek

Jarron
you came up to me, no introduction

Dana
I liked the look of you

Jarron
you liked the look of me?

Dana
is that so odd?
you said you worked for the UN, I was curious

Jarron
you were wearing practically nothing, underwear

Dana
it was a dress

Beat.

it was a dress

Jarron
  that was a dress?

Dana
  where do you come from?

Jarron
  I've seen dresses but really –
  I'm sorry. I made a mistake

Dana
  too right you did
  Christ alive. I can't believe you thought – Jesus

Jarron
  girls don't come up to me like you did.

Dana
  I'm not a girl
  my name is Dana
  I have a degree. I have a fucking mind which I can
  make up.

Dana sits up with the sheet about her knees.

Jarron
  so? I pay for sex, I thought everyone does

Dana
  not around here

Jarron
  they do where I come from

Dana
  and where the fuck is that
  hell?

He laughs.

  don't laugh

Jarron
well stop making jokes

Dana
I'm serious
sex that you pay for is toxic
an irritant, feels nice for a second but

Jarron
it suits me

Dana
you don't know any other way, you've forgotten any
other way

Jarron
yeah, maybe I have

Dana
then someone should show you

Beat.

I would offer but you just offended me. Seriously
offended

Jarron
I said I was sorry

Beat.

He is tempted for a second.

Then he pulls away.

you ought to wear more when you go out
you ought to be more careful about the message you
send

Dana
everyone wears stuff like that

He starts to put his trousers on.

where are you going?

Jarron
    I've got miles to drive today
    I have to get down to the Adriatic, over to North
    Africa

Dana
    and that's it?

Jarron
    well, what else is there?

Dana
    I made you an offer

Jarron
    which you then retracted

Dana
    okay, it's there. The offer.
    I'll make love to you because I want to.
    and you can make love to me, knowing that.

Beat.

Jarron
    I don't have time

Dana
    oh, it's scary –?

He looks at her.

Jarron
    you don't know me

Dana
    I didn't know you before

Jarron
    we talked for an hour in the bar we got shitfaced we
    screwed each other

Dana
we were tender we kissed

Jarron
stop it
fucking stop it

Dana
I can't believe this is so hard for you
it's two people, two consenting adults
don't worry you don't have to fall in love with me –

Jarron
I thought I knew what we were doing here
I thought we both knew what was going on, I thought
this was up and down, around and about, both
parties agreed all okay

Dana
it is okay

Jarron
no it's not fucking okay

Dana
of course it's okay

He reaches for his shirt.

you don't need to run quite so fast

Jarron
this doesn't happen to me.
I am a really powerful person, people don't trick me

Dana
I didn't trick you

Jarron
this is fucked up. This is really fucked up. I organise
people for a living, I write reports, I travel miles and

miles, people don't do this to me. I don't get caught
like this

Dana
you aren't caught

He does his buttons up.

Jarron
I don't drink with women in bars for real. You get it.

Dana
what is wrong with saying I like you, I think you're
nice

He puts his shoes on.

Jarron
nice? Do you want to know how not nice I am?
what if I tell you I only came with you because I could
see you had some goodness, I could see I could break
your heart

Dana
get over yourself
I came to you not the other way around

Jarron
I still ended up with my cock up your arse.

Beat.

I thought you would notice my semen is black, my
face twisting, my nails ridged, in short it didn't occur
to me you would do anything other than hold me in
contempt. I am unloveable, the unloved. Not the sort
of person that gets told they are nice. Feared maybe,
fucking hated, yes. I am a devil, I told you, a demon,
a thunderclap, I am a really fucking powerful person.
People cross the road to get out of my way, I am a
nightmare, an underpass in the dark, an alleyway, a
bridge that you don't cross.

Dana

I think I've got it.

Jarron

you fucking crazy bitch.

Dana

I didn't realise you were playing a game.
you should have said

Jarron

that would have ruined it.
fucking nice. You fucking load of shit.
don't give me nice

He has put his clothes on.

I've got to go. I've got a thousand miles to drive
today.

Dana

you already said that

He starts to go.

He comes back.

Jarron

I really think I should pay you.
I just think this will be cleaner if I give you something
I slept here after all. I'll give you something for the bed

Dana

I don't want anything

Jarron

you must want something. There is always something.
a new phone or another dress. Get yourself another
dress –
why won't you take my money?

Dana

why does it bother you?

Jarron
  alright. Alright, I get it. You're not desperate
  you are not for sale
  you think love can't be bought, admirable but slightly
  outdated, but still. I admire that.

Beat.

  I don't want this to be left messy, like either of us have
  any reason to even think about last night ever again.
  I have important things to think about, I don't want
  to think about you

Dana
  so don't think about me then

Jarron
  you'll want money in the end.

Dana
  I doubt it

Jarron
  I'm a fucking demon I told you. A god. I want to play
  fucky fucky with your head, it's done.

Dana
  what does that mean?

Jarron
  two weeks and you'll be begging me to pay you.

Dana
  I don't think so

He picks up his jacket.

Jarron
  bye bye Dana

Dana
I'm not scared of you, yes you've got a trumped-up
ego, but you've got no power.
what power have you got?

He goes out of the door.

we fucking used a condom.
don't try and scare me.

Dana is left alone.

fucking cretin.

She kicks out at the sheets.

moron.
oh god.

THREE

*Dana goes into a room where her sister is getting
dressed.*

Dana
I fucked a demon

Jasmine
you what?

Dana
I fucking fucked a demon.
all night long.

Jasmine
all night long?

Dana
yes
several times, lots of different ways. Oh shit, lots of
different ways

Her sister looks at her. Takes her in.

Goes back to brushing her hair.

Jasmine
well never mind

Dana
I'm being serious
he said he was from the UN

Jasmine
and was he?

Dana
I don't know

Jasmine
why do you do these things?

Dana
he looked nice. He stood at the end of the bar by the
window, I was carrying stuff past him, he moved out
of the way

Jasmine
you fucked him because he moved out of the way?

Dana
not just that, obviously, but it was a kind thing to do,
I was carrying all these bags and my laptop, there was
only a tiny space

Jasmine
are you completely desperate?

Dana
I thought maybe we would fall in love and live in each
other's arms
that was a joke by the way
I thought he might buy me a drink, light me a cigarette

Jasmine
for goodness sake

Dana
he could have tripped me up
he could have pushed me over, he could have spat in
my face

Jasmine
he could have done. Yes.
go and have a bath or something
forget him.

Dana stands at the window.

Dana
I tried that

Beat.

Jasmine
you're the one that is always telling me to move on,
flick a switch in your head and let him fall out the
back

Dana
and look what good that did you

Jasmine
I bet he didn't even leave his number.

Dana
he knows where I live, he might come back –
how far is the Adriatic?

Jasmine
the Adriatic?

Dana
that's where he is headed

Jasmine
Dana, stop this.

Dana
something happened between us

Beat.

I know how silly that sounds.

Beat.

Jasmine
aren't you supposed to be getting ready?

Dana
why?

Jasmine
hello

Dana
oh god

Jasmine
you hadn't forgotten?

Dana
what time is it?

Jasmine
ten to

Dana
shit

Jasmine
what has got into you?

Dana
I'll make it I'll make it
oh Christ

Jasmine
I'm not going to bring you coffee
I am not a waitress, a hand-maiden, I am not the

fucking mother, you forgot about it, okay. You can
deal with it

Dana starts to rush around looking for some clothes.

Dana
I can't believe this

Jasmine
where do you have to be anyway?

Dana
centre of town
where's my jacket?

Jasmine
I can't give you a lift either, I am not a taxi driver, a
chauffeur, you need a private secretary you get one
I'll ring you a taxi
my car's in the garage anyway so even if –

Dana
have you got a shirt I can borrow?

Jasmine
they're all creased

Dana
what about that one?

Jasmine
this one that I am wearing?

Dana
yes

Jasmine
this one I am wearing right now?

Dana
this is an emergency

Jasmine
it's a grant interview
let's be realistic

Dana
for a grant I really want

Jasmine
that you want so much you forgot the interview

Dana
please can I borrow your shirt?
I am your sister and I need some help

Jasmine
a sister yes, but not a dependant
unbelievable

Jasmine starts to take her shirt off.

So does Dana.

have my skirt as well, why don't you?

Dana looks at it.

Dana
no thanks

Jasmine
fucking cheek
I have a job as well you know

Dana
oh heck, I was going to polish my shoes

Jasmine
no time for that. Here.

Jasmine takes her shoes off and passes them to Dana.

Dana
you don't need them today?

Jasmine
I'm not doing anything that is life-critical, no. anything else?

Dana
my brain to be in gear

Jasmine
you're on your own there –

Dana takes her shirt off.

Underneath she has a mark.

Dana
I can't believe after all this work I would nearly forget the damn thing

Jasmine
what's that?

Dana
where?

Jasmine
under your bra

Dana
nothing

She looks.

nothing

Jasmine
what sort of sex did you have?

Dana
well, what is it –

Jasmine comes over and looks at her.

Jasmine
looks like a hicky

Dana
    oh

Jasmine
    from a *wolf*
    who was this guy?

Dana goes and looks in the mirror.

Dana
    do you think it's possible to fall in love at first sight?

Jasmine
    oh fucking hell

Dana
    I didn't say I loved him, just

She looks at the mark.

    just a hicky

Jasmine
    exactly
    leave it alone then

Dana looks again.

Dana
    what time is it?

Jasmine
    five to.

Dana
    alright
    how do I look?

Jasmine
    not bad

Dana
    I actually think I should get some cream

Jasmine
it's just a hicky

Dana
I know

Jasmine
please don't get a thing about a hicky, I know this
man spooked you

Dana
it's just a bit sore.
You know how my skin reacts

Jasmine
it probably wasn't even him.

Dana
exactly
it probably was there yesterday

Jasmine
well there you are then.

Dana
have you got some cream?

Jasmine
get some on the way home

Dana
what if he has done something to me?

Jasmine
there are no demons, right.

Dana
he said he was a god

Jasmine
there are no gods.
Dana, are you serious? A god. You believe in gods now?

Dana
his semen was black

Jasmine
    then fucking wash yourself.
    man's disgusting. Yuk.

Beat.

Dana
    I will.
    after my interview.
    how do I look?

Jasmine
    you'll knock them dead. You know that? You always do.

FOUR

Dana in her interview.

She sits on a chair, bathed in bright light.

The voices of several interviewers seem to come from all around her.

Interviewer 1
    Miss Dana Edwards?

Dana
    yes

Interviewer 2
    thank you for coming, Miss Edwards

Dana
    no problem

Interviewer 1
    we would like to go over some aspects of your
    application if you don't mind

Dana
    of course

Interviewer 3

when you said you would like to set up a research
group could you expound your area of expertise?

Dana

well I was working in a company and was trying to
improve on the customer experience, when I started
to read about something called Customer Dynamics,
which sounds rather dry but is actually a new and
exciting theory on customer–business relationships
that redefines interchange of information and
transactions using psychoanalytical modelling and
techniques, likening the customer–business contact
to other basic human interactions, such as love.

Beat.

sorry, such as lust
such as friendship. I mean friendship, I don't know
why I said that.
such as friendship, and if you were to apply the right
indices to a variety of different forms of friendship
after all –

Beat.

I'm sorry I seem to have lost my thread.
friendship, mutual outcomes working together, that is
the essence of what commerce is trying to persuade
the individual,
that the needs are mutual, when in fact of course they
are different but –
I meant to say such as found in original bartering-type
cultures. We find the roots of all financial transactions
in . . .

She comes to a stop again.

do you mind if I look at my notes?

Interviewer 2
take your time

Dana looks at her notes.

She puts them the right way up.

She feels a bit hot.

Dana
the research I am doing is to try to pinpoint every
human interaction into the same framework

Interviewer 3
you already said that.

Dana
I know I said that.
could we turn this light down, only it's shining right
in my eyes

Interviewer 2
we don't have a lot of time, Miss Edwards, we have
quite a few candidates to see today, I am sure you
appreciate

Dana
of course

She feels like an idiot.

She goes back to her notes.

She re-starts.

customer exchanges occur over a wide range of
communication channels, and there is no distinction in
these channels between other communications that the
customer might receive. You might in the same second
get a text from your partner, and then from your bank.
To maximise the feeling of mutuality, should the text
from your bank feel *more* on your team than from

your partner? It is *your* bank, there to listen to you.
It may take a role and a flavour, a character if you
like. I think with the right modelling Customer
Dynamics could go beyond the transactional nature of
the interaction to look at emotions, intent and desires.
If we start to view each interaction as a chain of
events with a narrative –

Beat.

She has come to a full stop.

oh, I see you are writing, I was wondering if you were
still listening.

Interviewer 2
we are just making some notes.

Dana
I wondered if I had bored you

Interviewer 1
sorry?

Dana
I just meant –
well it doesn't sound, I know it doesn't sound –
the people out there are here to study Milton. And
Dante and Goethe. They were telling me all this stuff
about poetry, about our understanding of –
well they can explain I didn't really get it but . . .
I wish you would turn these lights down I can't really
see you.

Interviewer 3
have you any other questions, Miss Edwards?

Beat.

Dana
sorry I didn't mean it is dull. I just meant, next to
poetry. It's important to our understanding though, of

course, crucial and could add so much to the sales of
an emerging business

Interviewer 1
thank you so much, Miss Edwards

Dana
I should have said that perhaps at the start. I think it's
important.

Interviewer 2
thank you

Dana
what about the rest of my presentation?

Silence.

She gets off the chair.

okay
okay I see
shit.

FIVE

The library on the way home.

*A Librarian, a tall gangly and deeply precise man, is
stacking books on some shelves.*

Dana
sorry. Can I speak to you?

Librarian
if you would like

Dana
I mean I won't disturb anyone

Librarian
this is a library, you have to be quiet

Dana
okay but I can talk?

Librarian
you can talk to me, you can't talk to your friends

Dana
that's okay, my friends aren't here. Just me.

She has tried to make a joke, it hasn't worked.

Beat.

I am looking for a book about demons

Librarian
we are about to close, I should warn you.

Dana
oh. Should I come back?

Librarian
what sort of demons?

Dana
I am not sure. I was wondering if there are pictures of demons in literature

Librarian
pictures in literature?

Dana
well pictures, obviously not pictures. Descriptions

Librarian
plenty.
where shall we start, Shakespeare, Proust?

Dana
Milton

Librarian
Milton?

Dana
does he have anything interesting to say about
demons?

Librarian
lots. Where do you want to start?

Dana
you tell me

Librarian
maybe you want to see our Milton specialist, they are
in on a Wednesday, I can make you an appointment

Dana
I'm really only browsing.

Librarian
browsing for demon literature?

Dana
yes.

Librarian
you don't have time to browse, we are about to close

Dana
okay, what about Dante? Goethe?

Librarian
you can't just say Dante / Goethe.
Literature is like the universe, a solar system. Dante
and Goethe are different planets. You can't dot about
like this, picking names from anywhere. We have to
start at the beginning. Era, context, meaning.

Dana
do you have any books that might help me?

Beat.

Librarian
what is your specific question?

Dana
my specific question?

Librarian
yes

Dana
alright
what happens if you piss one off?

Librarian
a demon?

Dana
yes
it's a hypothetical question

Librarian
I realise it is hypothetical, I am a librarian.

Dana
of course you are

Librarian
this is a library, the home of the hypothetical question

Dana
exactly

Librarian
have you pissed one off?

Dana
of course not.

Dana laughs.

The Librarian laughs.

Dana laughs again.

yes

Librarian
very funny

Dana
what would happen?

Librarian
a god or a demon?

Dana
both, either

Librarian
so something powerful?

Dana
yes

Librarian
that you pissed off?

Dana
yes

Librarian
lightning would strike I guess

Dana
in literature?

Librarian
in literature

Dana
can you be a bit more specific?

Librarian
can you?

Dana
alright, say the demon thinks he owes you a debt, but you didn't let him pay

Librarian
a demon wouldn't get into debt

Dana
well, say he did

Librarian
how could he?

Dana
just hypothetically say it had happened

Librarian
but we are talking about literature here, right?
we are taking our examples from literature,
so we only have the examples that other people have
written. It isn't like a phrase book

Dana
okay, I just thought there might be some guidance.
don't you think they are out there, they might be an
owner of a business or someone who robs you in the
street, or a father who is abusing someone

Librarian
it's a bit different

Dana
every age must have their equivalents.

Librarian
I only really know about literature
and –

Dana
the library is about to close

Librarian
exactly

Dana
I was just asking what literature said of pissing off
someone like that –

Librarian
in literature someone who classed himself as a demon
wouldn't like to have a debt. He will work really hard
to make sure he doesn't owe anyone anything. That is
the basis of selling your soul. Devil or demon, they are
the original transactional creature.

Dana
so if he did think he owed you something?

Librarian
he wouldn't
he would find a way to pay it

Dana
you seem very absolute about that?

Librarian
I don't know all of literature, I am mainly a classicist

Dana
I understand but what about a mark? Might they
leave some sort of IOU on you?

Librarian
like what?

Dana
I am talking hypothetically

Librarian
of course you are

Dana
because we're in a library
what if a demon were to leave a sort of a sore –

Librarian
on your body?

Dana
yes.

Librarian
I would have to look that up.

Dana
well could you look it up?

Librarian
now?

Dana
yes please

Librarian
I could but we are about to close.

Beat.

I could look it up in the morning but tomorrow is my day off. I could look it up on Tuesday if you like.

Dana
okay

Librarian
but if a demon left a sore on my body, I wouldn't like it. The mark of the devil, well it's not going to be good, is it?

Dana
isn't it?

Librarian
I wouldn't have thought so, no.

Dana
hypothetically

Librarian
hypothetically of course.

SIX

Dana

okay you've had your fun. Very funny. Fucking demon
I am talking to you. You want to scare me. You want
to get in my head – too bad. I can put cream on the
mark. You've infected me with something I'll take a
tablet. Bring it on, you want to send me your curses,
I'll bat them back. I am invincible, stronger than you,
surrounded with a shield, a force of my own. I will
knock you sideways. I will bowl you over, I will wrap
you in a knot and tie you in ribbons. What do you
think of that? Hey, nightmare, a dark alleyway, a man
with a knife, a pain that won't stop, a roaring fire, a
child's face howling, hunger, plague, disease
I'm not scared of you
I am not scared of anyone, and particularly not you.
you get in my head, I'll leave you there
you get in my body, I will caress you
you get in my hair I will curl it and put it up

Jarron appears sitting at a table having a beer.

Jarron

you want a drink?

Dana

where were you?

Jarron

I had some work to do. I came back, didn't I?

Dana

you came back here?

Jarron

I drove to the south, I did my work, I came back

Dana
why?

Jarron
we hadn't finished

Dana
hadn't we?

Jarron
no we hadn't and I didn't like it
this needs to be over and done with now. And quickly.

Dana
quickly?

Jarron
I'm presuming you would have changed your mind

Dana
about what?

Jarron
the cheque. I have written it out, and before you ask
no it's not sizeable.

Dana
oh that

Jarron
it's 45 euros which I think is an adequate
representation of the time taking into account the
distress you have caused me, the inconvenience of
having to return. I have charted it all, put my petrol
in, my time, the wear and tear on my car, and 45
euros left to you covers it I think.

Dana
is that right?

Jarron
if you want to make a different representation then we
can enter into a negotiation at the end of this meeting

Dana
this is a meeting?

Jarron
I am prepared to raise it slightly but only just. And
before you say there is no debt, there is a debt. There
is a big fucking debt, that is the only explanation

Dana
for what?

Jarron
for what has been happening with me since I saw you.
this sensation I have
this uncomfortable sensation,
why I can't control my thoughts as I should –
you are nothing, you are inconsequential, you aren't
even beautiful.
you don't make me laugh. Your dress sense is terrible.
Your teeth are crooked, your breath smells in the
morning, you are ugly in some lights, not as clever as
you think –

Dana
glad we've got that clear

Jarron
and you are a woman. Basically
you are a woman.
you aren't even nearly the sort of person I should be
thinking about.

Beat.

please take the money and release me.
I thought I knew every trick in the book, but there is
obviously one that got away.

Dana
I can't release you

Jarron
I'll pay you to undo it, how about that? 45 euros, it's not a payment for the other night, it's a payment for your unlocking services

Dana
and if I can't?

Jarron
find a way.

Dana
you want me to stop you from loving me?

Jarron
who talked about love?

Dana
that's the sensation you described

Jarron
it's not love

Dana
what is it?

Jarron
a curse of some kind.
you've made me obsessed by you

Dana
so you are obsessed?

Jarron
you fucking bitch, you don't have to smile

Beat.

this, this is over
you know that?

Dana
okay by me

286

Jarron
  things could get bad for you

Dana
  bring it on

Jarron
  why aren't you scared of me?

Dana
  because you aren't scary.
  you say you had your soul ripped out, but I can feel it
  still beating in the palm of my hand.

Jarron
  you'll take my money. In the end.

Dana
  what, and then you think you'll be free of me?

Jarron
  I'll forget you then, yes
  yes

Dana
  maybe

Jarron
  no good will come of this, you know that?

Dana
  we'll see.

SEVEN

Dana is at home.

Jasmine
  Dana?
  Dana? You were talking to yourself

Dana
was I?

Jasmine
how did it go?

Dana
badly.
actually.

Jasmine
really?

Dana
yes, really badly.
I fucked up
I thought I was prepared and then, Jesus why wasn't
I better prepared?

Jasmine
you were prepared –

Dana
I got in there, and all the stuff I had meant to say

Jasmine
why do you always do this?

Dana
do what?

Jasmine
say it's all dreadful, a disaster and make me believe
you have failed, and then –

Dana
not this time

Jasmine
they rang for fuck's sake.
when they got me they left a message. You impressed

them, you impressed them very much. You impressed
them so much they are putting you forward for an
international position

Dana
an international position?

Jasmine
they want you to go and talk to their colleagues in
Alexandria

Dana
what?

Jasmine
some sort of cross-university team

Dana
in Alexandria?

Jasmine
they said ring them in the morning

Dana
there must be a mistake

Jasmine
you bloody aced it

Dana
did they actually use my name, maybe they rang the
wrong candidate?

Jasmine
they're putting you forward for an international
award for Christ's sake
forget Berlin

Dana
they'll ring in the morning and say there's been an
error –

Jasmine
will you stop for once?
you got it. Hello?
you got it with bells on, you're going to fucking
Alexandria

Beat.

Dana
I don't understand it

Jasmine
what is there to understand?

Dana
then the other candidates must have been really poor
or stupid,
I promise you I fucked up

Jasmine
for god's sake –

Dana
why are you cross with me?

Jasmine
when I fuck up, I really fuck up. That's the difference.
When you fuck up, you still win.

Dana
how was your day?

Jasmine
no worse than normal.

Dana looks at her.

and I'll miss you like hell if you move to Alexandria

Dana
I haven't got it yet. Have I?
they just want me to talk to the people in Alexandria

Jasmine
you'll get it. Why wouldn't you?

Dana
maybe I don't even want it.
when do they want me there?

Jasmine
Monday

Dana
this Monday?

Jasmine
better start packing.

Beat.

Dana
we were going to do something together this weekend

Jasmine
doesn't matter

Dana
look at some flats, see about our deposit

Jasmine
we've got lots of weekends

Dana
not if I go to Alexandria

Jasmine
I can amuse myself for forty-eight hours, don't worry

Dana
can you?

Jasmine
I'm not completely useless, I've got work to do

Dana
I'll lock the fridge

Jasmine
I'm through that. Please.
I'm through that.

Beat.

Dana
I can't go to Alexandria for Monday

Jasmine
course you can

Dana
why don't you come too?

Jasmine
I've got so much to catch up on

Dana
bring it with you
have a few days away
we could get a train, see some of the coast

Jasmine
which coast?

Dana
I don't know, maybe the Adriatic
take a boat

Jasmine
why would we go to the Adriatic?

Dana
I am just talking about making it more of a trip
we always said we wanted to see more of Europe,
the sea
I was just thinking of ways to make it

Jasmine
what?

Dana
more fun

Jasmine
by going a thousand miles out of our way?

Dana
isn't that the basis of an adventure?

Beat.

Jasmine
he's a dick, you know that

Dana
who?

Jasmine
the man you were with. All men are dicks but he is a high-class representative of his species. Even Jerome said he was a dick and that is saying something

Dana
I wasn't talking about him

Jasmine
you told me he was headed for the Adriatic

Dana
did I?

Jasmine
and he's some kind of con man.
seriously, he is fucking dangerous. I went into the bar this morning, he didn't pay for all his drinks, tried to con the waitress, then left a credit card number that didn't work.

Dana
why are you telling me this?

Jasmine
because I think you're still thinking about him

Dana

that's ridiculous. Even if he was at the Adriatic, that
isn't an address, there must be a million people there

Jasmine

so that isn't why you would go that way?

Dana

absolutely not
the Adriatic is beautiful I've heard, and –
he was a passing moment. One night of something,
but in the cold light of day meaningless
and I don't want to see him again.
I can't see him again
how could I see him again?
thank god for you setting me right. Men like that,
who needs them?

Jasmine

maybe I should come with you –

Dana

you don't have to

Jasmine

a couple of days away

Dana

you'd be bored

Jasmine

keep you company

Dana

there are a million people in the Adriatic, how could
I find him?

Jasmine

it won't stop you trying
he works for the UN, that is a start

Dana
  I'll be fine

Jasmine
  I know, but as you say it's ages since I have been on a
  trip.

Dana
  really?

Jasmine
  you think you are the only person that can behave
  rashly?

Dana
  we only have one suitcase

Jasmine
  we can share
  we share everything else.

Dana
  it's a bit fucking hasty

Jasmine
  and you aren't?

Jasmine goes and gets the suitcase.

She puts it out in front of Dana.

Beat.

Dana
  I don't have to take a position thousands of miles
  away

Jasmine
  you might want to

Dana
  I'll just go to see

Jasmine
you can't live with your sister for ever
even I know that, this is a phase that one day will end

Dana
I like living with you

Jasmine
I tie you down

Dana
not at all.

Beat.

Jasmine
alright, you tie me down then

Dana
fuck off.

Jasmine
I'd be okay you know. Without you.

Dana
of course you would.

Beat.

Jasmine
why are you looking at me like that?

Dana
I'm not

Jasmine
I'm not a charity case, okay after Mum and Dad died,
but –

Dana
I know what is going on

Jasmine
how can you know?

Dana
I've guessed

Beat.

Jasmine
you guessed?

Dana
tell me I'm wrong.

Jasmine
if you've guessed why the hell didn't you say?

Dana
I was waiting for you to say something.

Jasmine
and what if I didn't?

Dana
you'd have to eventually

Jasmine
does it show?

Dana
only on your face.

Beat.

Jasmine
it shows on my face?

Dana
a bit.

Jasmine
alright. So you're the clever one. So tell me, what am I going to do? I'm on my own.

Dana

you're going to pack a bag and come with me to Alexandria, and we'll have the whole train journey to work that out.

Jasmine

I thought you'd be angry, I thought you'd stomp about and say how could I have been so stupid. I'm supposed to be a grown-up –

Dana

well, how could you have been so stupid?

Jasmine

I don't know. I have no fucking idea
well, I have some idea but in specifics, no, fuck knows

Dana

fuck did know

Jasmine

yes, fuck did know

Dana

was it Jerome?

Jasmine

I don't want to talk about who it was

Dana

Jerome

Jasmine

Dana –

Dana

pack your bag

Jasmine

are you sure?

Dana

two women and an unborn baby going to Alexandria. What could be better?

Jasmine smiles.

Jasmine

I am not a fucking sob story though. Promise me, this isn't a poor Jasmine thing?

Dana

no, it's a poor fucking Dana thing, I've got to put up with you. Puking, no – mood swings – give me strength.

EIGHT

Dana is back in the library.

The Librarian is there.

Dana

I wondered have you got any of those books that I ordered –

Librarian

we aren't open quite

Dana

it's nine o'clock

Librarian

not by my watch. It's a minute to

Dana

I have a train to catch –

Librarian

this is a council library. We have to do things the council's way

Dana

and that is?

Librarian

at the appointed time

Dana
my watch says nine

Librarian
it's my watch that counts
and the clock on the wall, the library clock

Dana
alright, but maybe I could just talk to you while –

Librarian
fifty-one, fifty-two
you see the second hand

Dana
I don't want to miss my train

Librarian
fifty-seven, fifty-eight. Fifty-nine
can I help you?

Dana
I came in before.

Librarian
oh yes
about the mark

Dana
not just the mark

Librarian
the demon I remember, you –
you ordered every book in the entire city's collection
on devils, marks, sexually transmitted marks, whether
they have AIDS in hell, they haven't come in yet, sorry

Dana
what?

Librarian
you overloaded the system, it will be a day or two

Dana
I can't wait a day or two

Librarian
well next time just order one book not nine hundred

Dana
you are sure there is nothing?

Librarian
there is one thing

Dana
yes

Librarian
it appears we overcharged you
there's a small note on your file

Dana
that can't be right –

Librarian
you had a few fines a couple of years back, and it says
here that you paid them, but going through it looks
like we owe you a rebate

Dana
a rebate? I've never been in the library before

Librarian
says here

Dana
must be a mistake

Librarian
45 euros is the number that is coming up.
I can pay you now if you like

Dana
oh I see

Librarian
I could write a cheque or just give you the cash

Dana
I knew it was you

Librarian
I'm sorry

Dana
of course you would keep trying. I should have thought.
put it away I told you I won't take it

Librarian
alright, we could do a bank transfer

Dana
I know this is a test, you can test me all you want, I won't fail,
overcharged me for a non-existent library fine, you'll have to do better than that

Librarian
excuse me

Dana
I'm no fool, I am on to you and your tricks
devil

Librarian
listen, lady

Dana
black semen ridged nails

Librarian
now wait a minute

Dana
scar on your chest where they tore your soul out

Dana pushes him.

Librarian
I would rather you didn't do that

Dana
stop it, you stop it right now
stop pretending

She grabs him.

Librarian
would you mind taking your hands off me?

Dana
not until you admit it's you

Librarian
admit I'm who?

They fight.

She rips his shirt.

He is pushed over on the library floor.

Dana
no scar?

Librarian
who on earth do you think you are?

Dana
you aren't him?

Librarian
who? The demon?

Dana
sorry

Librarian
you thought I was the demon?

Dana
I mistook you

Librarian
I was actually trying to help you
I was trying to be nice
the council doesn't often hand out rebates.
you should be so blessed.

He gets up.

insanity. The first symptom of possession.

Dana
I am not insane

Librarian
thinks they have a mark

Dana
I have a mark

Librarian
it's in your mind

Dana
what is this then?

She lifts up her T-shirt.

Librarian
that's it?

Dana
yes

Librarian
it looks like a mosquito bite

Dana
it hurts

She covers herself up with her shirt.

it hurts a lot
and it's getting bigger.

Librarian
I suggest cream then.

Dana
brilliant

Librarian
antiseptic cream.

Dana
I could have thought of that myself, how helpful

Librarian
helpfulness, that's what I am here for.

Dana starts to go.

you know I once fucked a demon

Dana
excuse me?

Librarian
don't think that you are the only person that has
taken that road. Uncomfortable and gorgeous all at
the same?
regrettable and delicious. It was many moons ago, but
I remember it well.
run run, you've got a train to catch.

NINE

Dana and Jasmine are on the train.

Dana
I just think it's a general principle, you shouldn't let
people give you money. Even the council. Not unless
you want it. Not unless you ask for it. I hadn't asked
for it. In fact I had specifically said

Jasmine
this is a general principle?

Dana

we don't know who he was, he said he was a librarian. He worked in a library, so what? He could have been anyone

Jasmine

well, we know who he wasn't

Dana

men in particular. I don't think we should be taking money from men, and keep your guard, Jasmine, don't let people push money into your hand saying it is for me.

Jasmine

it's like you are at war

Dana

I am

Jasmine

over what?

Beat.

you know there is no such thing as a demon, right?

Dana

yes

Jasmine

glad we've got that clear

Beat.

Dana

but if there was such a thing, it would be just like him to change his appearance and become other people. You said he was a con man –

Jasmine

I can't do this. I can't go on a trip with you if you are going mad.

I am the one that has hormones rushing through my body. If anyone is entitled to go mad it is me.

Dana
go mad then.

Beat.

Jasmine
I did go mad. I came with you

Dana laughs a bit.

oh, you can still laugh?

Jasmine laughs a bit.

Dana laughs a lot.

there's supposed to be a nice bar on the main square and we've got an hour at Budapest station

Dana
sounds good

Jasmine
get a bloody great bottle of wine –

Dana
you shouldn't be drinking

Jasmine
I haven't decided anything yet

Dana
we'll buy a bottle and I'll end up drinking it all

Jasmine
and?

Dana
I have to give a presentation on Monday
I have to be sharp, together

Jasmine
you're going to end up a professor, aren't you?
you're going to end up one of those really smart
people that has written lots of books

Dana
I still won't earn as much as you –

Jasmine
I don't earn a lot. I earn a normal amount.

The Train Inspector comes along.

Inspector
there is actually a problem with your card

Dana
what sort of problem?

Inspector
the card you used to buy the tickets with, the bank's
refused it.

Dana
that's impossible

Inspector
you'll either have to get off at the next station or pay
again

Dana
are you serious?

Inspector
that's the rules, I'm sorry to say

Jasmine
wait a minute, could you try the card again?

Inspector
if it's already been refused –

Jasmine
sometimes the phone lines get twisted, try again

The Inspector takes Dana's card.

The machine doesn't seem to like it.

are you using the right PIN?

Dana
don't be a moron

Dana punches in her PIN.

It doesn't work.

She takes the card out.

She kind of waves it around for a second.

She puts it back in.

Jasmine
try mine

She gets her card out.

Inspector
thank you

The Train Inspector puts the card in.

He hands the card machine to Jasmine.

Jasmine puts her PIN number in.

The card comes back out.

Jasmine
now that is ridiculous

Dana
it has to be your machine

Inspector
don't worry, you can get off at the next station and
ring your bank

Dana
we can't get off at the next station

Jasmine
we are trying to get to Athens then across to
Alexandria

Inspector
you're travelling without a ticket
that's an offence, sorry to say

Dana
how much cash have you got, maybe we could get
singles

Jasmine
I haven't got much cash on me

Inspector
two singles to Budapest, 90 euros

Dana
how much have you got, Jasmine?

Jasmine
I'm just looking
sixteen, eighteen

Dana
I've got another ten

Jasmine
thirty-six, I didn't think we'd need it

Dana
it's not enough.

Jasmine
is there someone we could phone?

Inspector
sometimes there are some deals
see what you can get to

She looks in her purse again.

Jasmine
I might have, yes another five
forty-one

Inspector
if you could make it to 45, you could have a two-for-
one offer

Jasmine
sounds good, another three –

Dana
what two-for-one offer?

Inspector
technically not official till next month, but I can bend
the rules a little

Dana
you'd give us a free ticket?

Inspector
they're only singles and you'd have to sort yourself
out when you change at Budapest, but –

Dana
sorry we can't take them

Jasmine
what?

Dana
we aren't taking his made-up offer
I know what this is

Jasmine
Dana, you are really fucking crazy, do you know that

Dana
I told you, we don't take money

Jasmine
it isn't money

Dana
it's 45 euros

Jasmine
it isn't actual cash

Inspector
only do you want it?

Dana
no

Jasmine
yes
excuse me.
I can't do this, I can't do this.

Dana
you do what you want, I'm not taking his money

Jasmine
it's not his money

Dana
you go on then, I'll get off, sort the bank and meet
you in Budapest

Jasmine
what, you would leave me?

Dana
it's a city, you'd be fine in a city. No fridges

Jasmine
fuck off

Inspector
I am sorry I am going to have to ask you to leave
the train

either that or I will have to phone the police to escort
you

Dana
fine, I've got it

Jasmine
Dana
I'm sorry about this

Inspector
only there's the rest of the train I need to see to

Jasmine
can you give me one ticket to Budapest please?

Dana
you'd leave me?

Jasmine
you've gone mad
yes I would.

The Inspector gives Jasmine a ticket.

The Inspector goes.

Dana and Jasmine look at each other.

Jasmine is flicking her ticket.

Dana
where the hell is the next place anyway?

Jasmine
Hartenharten

Dana
Hartenharten, that's a place?

Jasmine
shit happens, Dana, why does your life have to be so
elaborate, so fucking dramatic? It is all some conspiracy,

some ordained way of putting you in the centre of the
universe. Our cards got refused, so what?

Beat.

Dana
you don't get it

Jasmine
damn right I don't.

Beat.

so will I meet you in Budapest or not?

Dana
don't look at me like that

Jasmine
did you use a condom?

Dana
of course I did.

Jasmine
for every hole?

Beat.

stupid cow

Dana
you don't go mad from an STD

Jasmine
oh, so you admit you are mad now.
what is black semen anyway, some kind of blood
thing?

Dana
I don't know

Jasmine
did you actually see his semen, or did he just tell you
that?

Dana
do we have to talk about this so loudly?
everybody already is looking

Jasmine
how is the hicky?

Dana
I know, how about a loudhailer?
it grew into a boil then it burst yellow pus

Jasmine
are you serious?

Dana
I'm joking.
of course it didn't

Jasmine
oh, excuse me for saying anything, you just screwed a
man with black semen that you think is a devil –

Dana
it got quite big, I put cream on it

Jasmine
glad to see you can see the humour in this.
that's the station. By the way.
your stop.

Dana
what?

Jasmine
Hartenharten

Dana
where the hell is that even?

Jasmine
it's here.

Dana

okay, I'll meet you tonight.
Budapest station.

Jasmine

well what time?

Dana

as soon as I can. I'll ring you.
I'll be on the next train

She picks up the suitcase.

who takes the suitcase?

Jasmine

don't be so fucking stupid, you know I'll come with you.
you drive me crazy you know that?

TEN

Dana is giving part of her presentation.

Dana

I thought I would take a recent example. Customer
transactions. I am going to subtitle this section of my
presentation, 'How to still be civil when something
goes wrong'. You see just a day or so ago, I was on a
train and there was something wrong with my card.
Now the usual situation is that in the inspector's mind
the customer quickly changes from a would-be
positive collaborator on our shared enterprise of
paying and experiencing a pleasant-as-advertised
journey to some kind of criminal, eager to see the
company diddled, whereas in the customer's mind
they are still simply trying to pay. But in this instance,
this sort of interaction – the rules appeared to shift –

The Librarian taps her on the shoulder.

Librarian
I have those books you ordered

Dana
what are you doing here?

Librarian
I'm in Hartenharten for the weekend
I work in Hartenharten on the weekends
we have a pretty good library, and as you see it's open.

Dana
I didn't know there was a library

Librarian
you have brought yourself here
you walked right in the door
the rest of Hartenharten shuts at five, but we are open
more or less all the time

Dana
you live in Berlin. I saw you in Berlin only this morning

Librarian
this is like my other job, and look some of your books
are on these shelves, so we might as well –

Dana
are you following me?

Librarian
why would I follow you?
listen, don't knock it, I'm trying to help you. Last time
I just about got pulverised for it, luckily I am resilient.
And ever-helpful. The true librarian to the end. If you
don't want these books I can just put them back on
the shelves for you, or you can fill out a little yellow
slip for reserved.

Dana
okay I'll take them

The Librarian passes Dana a couple of books.

Librarian
first things first, a guidebook to Hartenharten,

Dana
I didn't ask for that

Librarian
maybe not, but I put in a few extras and believe me you'll need it. The illustrations are very good although it comes to the conclusion of many, don't stay here long. My advice pretty much concurs with that for what it's worth, get back on a main-route train as fast as you can. My second suggestion is a 'how to' book. Always the best, you can't go wrong with a 'how to' book. This one, *How to Live with No Money*, published a few years ago but still one of the classics.

Dana
what do you mean, no money?

Librarian
I mean not much money.

Dana
we have lots of money

Librarian
look, do you want these books or not?

Dana
we have lots of money in our bank account
we just need a bank

Librarian
third, *How to Survive an Economic Disaster*. Bit outdated, but –

Dana
if you could just tell me where the bank is

Librarian

fourth book. *How to Find a Bank when They Have All Shut*

Dana

why have they shut?

Librarian

do you read the papers? Watch the news?

Dana

what has happened?

Librarian

it was on the cards for a while, if you care to read Jefferson's *Economic Reality in Post-euro Europe* you would have had it all predicted. Or Fresherman's *How the Early Twenty-first-Century Economists Got it All Wrong*
the banks have shut their doors
internal collapse, one after the other
just like before. Only they have done it again

Dana

they were fine yesterday

Librarian

they were teetering yesterday. They weren't fine yesterday. If you read the small print, the detail of what was going on
look do you want these books or not?

Dana takes the books.

Librarian

don't bother to thank me

Dana

thank you.

She looks at the books. There are quite a few.

will the bank be open tomorrow?

Librarian
unlikely, did you hear what I said?

Dana
so, what? Is there a hotel we can stay in for the night?

Librarian
out the library, turn left. Metropole Street. Probably listed in the guidebook under places to particularly avoid but there isn't another one. Don't eat the breakfast, sleep with the lights on. Don't use the bath unless you are carrying disinfectant with you.

Dana
why are you looking after me?

Librarian
I'm not.
I'm looking after me.

Dana
where am I headed?

Librarian
don't ask.

ELEVEN

The hotel in Hartenharten.

Dana and Jasmine stand in their hotel room with their suitcase.

Jasmine
I knew we should have got a plane.

Beat.

Dana
it's not bad

Jasmine
it's not good

Dana
it's a bit cold.

Jasmine
it's fucking freezing.
one night?

Dana
yes
one night

Jasmine
it's so cold I can feel my bones

Dana
there must be some heating.

Jasmine
the windows don't even shut

Dana
we'll stuff them with clothes.

Beat.

it's just one night.

Jasmine
I know

Dana
I agree it's not great, is that a heater?

Jasmine
I think it was.

Dana
sit down I'll put the kettle on.

Jasmine sits down.

Jasmine
you know I'm crap at the cold

Dana
you'll be fine

Jasmine
there is cold and there is cold.
what if we wake up and we are frozen?

Dana
you've got the baby to keep you warm

Jasmine
poor ice-covered little thing

Dana
maybe you should stay with the suitcase and I'll go
and look for the bank

Jasmine
you just looked for a bank

Dana
well there must be another bank.
okay so one shut their doors but there must be another
one. They are all connected.

Jasmine
I live in the real world, Dana. They shut their doors
they shut their doors. I thought it wasn't supposed to
happen again.

Beat.

Dana
tea?

Jasmine
yes please.

Dana starts the kettle.

Dana
that will warm you up.
oh fuck, the kettle doesn't work

Jasmine
Jesus.

Beat.

no one loses all their money overnight, do they?

Dana
I guess not

Jasmine
there are regulations for this kind of thing, when
banks close, people are okay?

Dana
yes or they have been in the past

Jasmine
exactly everyone was okay last time, weren't they? The
countries were screwed but the individuals were okay.

Dana
I guess so

Jasmine
so we'll be fine then –

Dana
I need to get to Alexandria for Monday

Jasmine
so there are the big things like whether we have just
been bankrupted and then there are the small things
like whether we can get to Alexandria for Monday

Dana
it isn't a small thing

Jasmine
no but it isn't like losing all one's savings.

Dana

you've got the car

Jasmine

yes if we can get home, I've got the car.

Dana

I need to get to Alexandria, without this grant –

Jasmine

you'll get to Alexandria
we have what, forty-eight hours, we could walk if we
have to.

Dana

hardly

Jasmine

it's a setback, yes.
we are temporarily suspended.
do you think we are going to actually be able to sleep
here?
I mean I don't want to be fussy but
oh fucking hell

Beat.

She takes a deep breath.

what we need is an embassy. We're Europeans. We'll
go to the embassy tomorrow and tell them what has
happened, okay? This sort of thing happens, all the
time. No one actually loses money. They sort it

Dana

and in the meantime?

Jasmine

there is no meantime, this will be sorted.
bit of a pisser that we have to stay here tonight, but
basically –

Dana
what will we eat?

Jasmine
what?

Dana
aren't you hungry?
we haven't eaten anything since lunch

Jasmine
do you have to always turn to the problems?

Dana
we need to eat something don't we?
you are pregnant

Jasmine
and we will eat, we'll eat food

Dana
you spent all our euros on that stupid ticket, and we
haven't even paid for this room –

Jasmine
when we go to the embassy we will explain we need
some petty cash to tide us over. We won't be the only
people in this boat. I told you.

Dana
there isn't an embassy

Jasmine
there'll be one in the next town

Dana
that's quite a walk

Jasmine
we'll ring ahead. Make an appointment, then when
we get there they'll give us a temporary chequebook
or something. A small amount of money. We'll go to
the top of the queue because of the baby

Dana

I've got the bread from lunch

Jasmine

there you are then
we're fine

Dana

tomorrow is a Saturday
the embassy won't be open on a Saturday
and the next day is Sunday

Jasmine

we'll go Monday

Dana

I have to be in Alexandria on Monday

Jasmine

well, maybe in an emergency they will open the
embassy even on a Saturday. I think this is an
emergency, don't you? All the major banks in Europe
folding at once.
there'll be a number. An information sheet.
someone will be printing up an information sheet and
delivering them to all the hotels right now.

Dana

okay.

Jasmine

even in Hartenharten
the information sheets will get through.

Beat.

have you got any other food? Other than the bread?

Dana

for tomorrow?

Jasmine

not specifically for tomorrow, I just wanted to know

Dana
I feel a bit hungry now

Jasmine
that's the panic
you can't panic in a situation like this

Dana
what if we get really hungry in the night and we want
to eat all the food?

Jasmine
I'm through that, I told you

Dana
you're pregnant, anything could happen

Jasmine
don't turn this into I am the one who is fucking it up

Dana
okay calm down

Jasmine
if one of us wakes up in the night and eats all the food
it will be a bit of a bugger, but not a disaster because
we are both well-nourished and even a pregnant
woman can walk to the embassy in the next town
with no breakfast.

Dana
okay

Jasmine
okay
what else have you got?

Dana
not much
couple of bananas I think
some emergency contraception
some chocolate

Jasmine

there you are then – riches. I bet you could live on a packet of wine gums for a week if you had to.

Dana gets it out.

Dana

why are you so calm?

Jasmine

because we live in Europe, because nothing really bad happens. We both have jobs, the worst of this is, is a bit of an inconvenience and perhaps not such a good mini-break but really in the grand scheme of life, not so bad.

Dana

my phone is about to run out of charge

Jasmine

so charge it

Dana

I forgot the charger

Jasmine

what?

Dana

well, we packed in a hurry. If we had a week to make lists and think about the sort of things we might need it's normally you that remembers things like a charger

Jasmine

alright, when we get things sorted out, we'll get a charger

Dana

perfect

Jasmine

we have plenty of money after all. All our inheritance plus savings.

this is just a temporary situation.
you are the one that knows about customer relations.
There will be a number to call, won't there?

Dana

probably.

Jasmine

some way that the bank will have of smoothing this
over

Dana

if the bank is bust, technically it won't be the bank

Jasmine

alright, whoever's job it is to make this okay. They
will make it smooth.

Dana

that fucking demon

Jasmine

I'm tired
I'm so fucking tired. Please.
we've been travelling all day

Beat.

Dana

you're tired of me

Jasmine

I'm tired of this.
I'm tired generally, but yes, I am tired of you.
do you mind if I go to sleep?

Dana

I'm sorry

Jasmine

aren't you tired?
I know the beds are crap and the room like the Arctic
but

Dana
 I'm not pregnant

Jasmine
 lucky you.

Jasmine starts to go to sleep.

Dana stays up.

She turns down the light.

Dana
 goodnight.
 I love you.

Jasmine
 love you too.

Dana
 I'm sorry

Jasmine
 don't be sorry, it's a fucking adventure.
 we'll laugh one day.

Dana
 very funny

Jasmine
 we will.
 when this child is born, we'll tell it about this hideous
 place we came to on the way to Alexandria

Dana
 when this child is born?

Jasmine
 yes, right before you got the most amazing job

Dana
 and right before you and the baby came out with me
 to live in Alexandria,

Jasmine
and right before we got this really nice flat because
you became a professor, and we'll tell the baby, that
life was pretty okay but we did have to spend one
night in a fridge

Dana
it will laugh and ask how can you live in a fridge
when a fridge is so small

Jasmine
ah, okay, we'll go not literally a fridge but a room
that was so cold you could see the ice forming

Dana
you should have been a poet

Jasmine
fuck off I'm going to sleep

Dana
that sounds nice by the way

Jasmine
what does?

Dana
talking to your baby.
when it's born

Jasmine
goodnight.

Dana
goodnight.

Dana looks around.

She opens her shirt and looks at the hicky.

She puts her hand up to it, it's sore to touch now.

All over her breast.

She turns round, it's all over her back too.

She takes a scrubbing brush to it.

TWELVE

Dana is in the bath.

The water is cold, but she doesn't notice.

In the bath with her is the demon.

He is sitting behind her and scrubbing her back.

Dana
surprise surprise

Jarron
what does that mean?

Dana
I knew you wouldn't stay away

Jarron
you're imagining me

Dana
whatever you say

Jarron
I'm a version in your head

Dana
okay by me.

Jarron
a weird version as it turns out
not quite me at full force
I would never get into a bath with a girl

He gets out of the bath and starts drying himself with a towel.

Jarron
  what do you want?

Dana
  I don't want anything

Jarron
  so why am I here?

Dana
  you brought yourself

Jarron
  in your dreams

Dana
  alright, I want to know why you are doing this?
  I mean I know what you are trying to do, I just want
  you to say it

Jarron
  you think I did this?

Dana
  didn't you?

Jarron
  what does your sister say?

Dana
  she didn't meet you

Jarron
  just take the damn thing, then it wouldn't really
  matter what the banks were doing, you could get to
  where you need to go

Dana
  we've been through this.

Jarron
  a nice 45-euro-worth hamper of food

Dana
no thank you

Jarron
think of your sister
pregnant after all. That poor little baby

Dana
my sister has nothing to do with it

Jarron
and freezing cold
how about a radiator, or a hot-water bottle to put at
her feet?

Dana
this is between you and me
you keep her out of it

Jarron
I am a demon, I don't have any morals, any
boundaries. I can go sideways I can go up I can go
down. I can punish your great-granddaughter for this,
or your aged ancestor.
it's all a bit silly isn't it, for a principle? For pride?
for your ego, for putting yourself first.
you can name your price, if crisp banknotes aren't
your thing
two return tickets to Alexandria

Dana
we'll get to Alexandria

Jarron
you need that job
Berlin is more or less collapsing
Europe is in the shit

Dana
Europe will pull together

Jarron
  we'll see

Dana
  are you going to kill me?

Jarron
  I am doing nothing
  I might do something about the temperature, aren't
  you cold?

Dana
  this on my neck

Jarron
  what about it?

Dana
  what is it?

Jarron
  it's nothing

Dana
  why is it growing?

He shrugs.

Jarron
  maybe you should go to a doctor

Dana
  you put it there so that I would have to come back
  to you
  so I would come and find you

Jarron
  here's the thing: I don't care

Dana
  so you keep saying

335

Jarron
I care nothing about you
if I did before, it's gone now

Dana
so why are you here?

Jarron
I'm not.

Pause.

They look at each other.

He shrugs and looks at her again.

I'm not

He can't quite break away though. They stare at each other.

They are almost irresistibly drawn to each other.

Then the moment is broken.

Some music starts up in the background.

what is that?

Dana
the next-door room

Jarron
can't you stop it?

Dana
probably not

Jarron
can't you ring down and get them to shut up?

Dana
what's wrong with it?

Jarron
it's music, it's fucking music

Dana
what is wrong with music?

Jarron
I don't like it, it plays with my head

Dana
you are by the telephone –

Jarron
alright

He picks up the telephone.

Dana comes and sits beside him, right at his back.

He arches his back to her touch.

don't do that

Dana
it's in my head, I'm not doing anything

She twists and puts an arm around him.

He is drawn to her.

Jarron
I said stop

Dana
you stop

Jarron
you stop first

He can't stop himself.

He twists and grabs her.

It's unclear if he is holding her or hurting her.

They fight for a second.

They roll, they kiss.

For a second or two it's irresistible.

Then he breaks away.

> you can't have this
> you can't have this version of me
> this isn't how it is
> this isn't how I am
> you are fucking twisting with my head now

Dana
> turns out I am stronger than you.

Jarron
> sorry, not true

He slaps her.

She holds her face.

He slaps her again.

She slaps him.

He grabs her again.

She grabs him.

He looks at her.

He tries to look at her very soul.

He throws her down.

> I'm going
> you won't see me again

Dana
> so we can go back to normal, we can use our bank
> card?

Jarron
  the banks have got nothing to do with me, I told you

Dana
  bollocks

Jarron
  goodbye, Dana

Dana
  I don't think it's goodbye

Jarron
  it will get pretty lonely, you know that.
  pretty hard from here
  you think you are cushioned, well, it is paper-thin.
  Doesn't it feel draughty already?

Dana
  someone will help us

Jarron
  do you think?

Dana
  as long as there are people there is some kind of
  civilising influence

The demon laughs at that. Long and hard.

I'll keep looking for you

Jarron
  you do that

Dana
  this isn't over between you and me

He eats the chocolate.

  don't eat the chocolate

He eats another bit.

we only have that for tomorrow

Jarron
you said bring it on

Dana
don't

He laughs again.

He eats more chocolate, and the bread.

don't touch the bread

Jarron
you'll have to tell her it was you.

Dana
leave her something.

He crams it into his mouth.

Jarron
why should I? I'm a god, I told you. I am the unclean.
The damned. I am the fucking nightmare.

Dana
where are you?
where will I find you?

He shrugs.

Jarron
I work for the UN.

THIRTEEN

Dana is too hot in her bed.

The Librarian is giving her books. He is fanning himself.

Librarian

*How to Get to Sleep in a Room that is Now Too Hot.
How to Turn a Heating System Down in a Room
without Air Conditioning.* A classic actually. *How to
Get to Sleep Despite the Extreme Heat.* Very useful,
but the spine is a bit worn now. I could see if there is
another copy. Did you check to see if the windows
opened? Or perhaps this one. *How to Dream when
You Aren't Sure You Are Asleep. How to Stay Asleep
and Still Even if it Feels Like You Are in an Oven,* a
bit outdated but you could try it. *How to Ignore the
Sweat Running Down Your Face, Dry Eyes.* They're
really amazing these 'how to' books. They have got a
title for almost anything. *How to Lie Awake and Not
Breathe in the Air*

Dana

where's Jasmine?

Librarian

How to Wash in Hardly Any Water. Not particularly
recommended, but you never know

Dana

Jasmine?

Librarian

*What to Wear for a Ten-mile Trek. How to Make a
Water Bottle from an Old Pair of Socks,* that doesn't
sound right –

Dana

where is Jasmine?

Librarian

How to Find Your Sister
oh hang on, wait a minute. There was one written just
like this
How to Find Your Sister when She is in Despair

Dana
why is she in despair?
okay so the food went but –
why is she in despair?

Librarian
it doesn't say.
it was just the title of a book. Do you want it or not?

Dana
I can't carry all these books.

Librarian
it's alright, that's why you have me. I carry them for
you.

Dana
why is Jasmine in despair?

Librarian
I don't have a title for that. Sorry.

FOURTEEN

Outside.

Jasmine is sitting on a bench.

Dana comes and sits beside her.

Dana
you could have left me a note
you could have left something to tell me where you
were going. I was worried. The room was so hot,
I woke up, no sign of you
went downstairs to see about the heat. No one at
reception.
went outside; nothing.
back to our room, worried now.
checked the toilet

Beat.

 I know you are mad
 you've a right to be but you didn't have to scare me
 just shout, scream. I know that food was all we had,
 and I know I have got at you for years for not being
 able to control yourself –

Beat.

 I don't know what came over me
 I'm not sure I was actually awake
 please don't be full of despair. We'll get some more
 food
 we'll find the embassy.

Jasmine
 I'm not cross

Dana
 you must be hungry, I mean I understand you have a
 little person in there

Jasmine
 I'm bleeding

Dana
 what?

Jasmine
 there's blood all over my pants

Dana
 Jesus, when?

Jasmine
 a few hours ago it started. The room got so airless,
 I sat up in the bed
 I felt something cool
 I put my hand down

Dana
oh god

Jasmine
my blood was actually cooler than the room, I
thought what is this cool stuff on my thighs?

Dana
Jesus

Jasmine
so much of it
Dana, there was so much of it
then of course as more and more came it got hotter
only a tiny person, how could there be so much?

Dana
why are you sitting here, we need to get you help

Jasmine
I think it's gone

Dana
you don't know that

Jasmine
the amount of blood, I don't see –

Dana
stand up, you need some help

Jasmine
I don't know what to do, Dana, you'd think I would
know what to do

Dana
you haven't lost it yet
you just need some help that's all
you might just need a tablet

Jasmine
yes a tablet, maybe there's a tablet –

Dana
I'll get you a doctor

Jasmine
how will you get a doctor here?

Dana
there'll be a doctor

Jasmine
oh fucking hell –

Dana
you hang on, everything will be fine
we'll be telling that baby all about this one day I
promise.

Jasmine
it's starting to hurt

Dana
I need some help. Help. Let go of my hand, I'll go to
the hotel, they can ring a doctor. Stand up

Jasmine
I can't stand up

Dana
sit then, I won't be long –

FIFTEEN

Dana
No NO NO NO NO. Alright. Alright, you win.
Hands up. You are bigger than me. I got the message.
You win. I'll take your money, I'll do whatever. Don't
do this to Jasmine and her baby. This has nothing to
do with Jasmine.
oi, where are you? Come back.

I said I'll take your money.
it was just sex. Lust. Nothing happened.
the devil can't be tamed by love. You stay all
powerful.
give me your fucking money.
where are you?
where are you?

A Woman is on the phone and talking to Dana.

Woman
I'm sorry I didn't catch that, what service do you
require?

Dana
ambulance.

Woman
it's a bad line, could you repeat?

Dana
ambulance. Ambulance, fucking ambulance

Woman
alright

Dana
how long before it gets here?

Woman
I need to do an assessment first

Dana
what sort of assessment? It's my sister, she's losing a
baby

Woman
is she breathing?

Dana
of course she is breathing, she is bleeding, that is the
thing

346

Woman
has she had a knock on the head?

Dana
no. Please just send the ambulance

Woman
chest pains?

Dana
she's losing a baby, didn't you hear me?

Woman
has she developed a headache or started slurring her words?

Dana
no, she is bleeding, she is bleeding a lot

The Librarian comes up to her with more tomes.

Librarian
How to Hold Your Sister's Hand when You Think She is Slipping Away.

Dana
I don't need a book, I just need an ambulance

Librarian
actually that is just a paper in a journal.

Woman
has she travelled overseas in the last three months?

Dana
no. No she hasn't.

Librarian
How to Count Someone's Heartbeat Even Though You Can Only Hear Your Own.

Woman
the ambulance is just being prepared

Dana
it doesn't need to be prepared, it just needs to get here

Librarian
are you still interested in these 'how to' books,
sometimes I think they go too far.

Dana
give them to me

Woman
should be with you shortly

Dana
how shortly? How long will it take?

Librarian
How to Stay Calm in Moments of Duress. Rather
straightforward to my mind, but nicely written

Dana
How to Call the Devil Back, have you got that?

Woman
there's been an incident in the town centre, you're in
a queue

Dana
what kind of queue?

Librarian
the e-books take a while, how are you spelling devil?

Dana
are you serious? Where is he? Get him back. I'll take
his money

Librarian
How to Find an Ambulance in Hartenharten, no you
have already done that

Woman
twenty minutes now

Dana
twenty minutes, there must be a way to call a devil

Librarian
you can't rush me
How to Keep Your Cool when Your Sister is Dying

Dana
she isn't dying
can you get it any quicker than twenty minutes?

Librarian
she doesn't get blood, she'll die

Dana
they'll give her blood then, won't they? Someone give
her some blood. Give me a book, *How to Make Them
Give Someone Blood when They Need Blood*

Librarian
How to Listen when People are Talking Nonsense

Dana
what sort of nonsense?

Woman
I am sorry I have to ask, do you have insurance?

Dana
insurance?
this is an emergency –

Librarian
How to Keep your Cool when Life is Stressful

Dana
– I don't need insurance

Woman
do you intend to pay for her treatment in cash?

Librarian
it's got a CD, this one with breathing exercises
meditation

Dana

Yes, we'll pay. I'll pay, whatever. I'll get you money. I thought this was Europe

Woman

it is Europe but the hospital now only takes cash

Librarian

How to Catch Up with the Times as They Change

Dana

I don't have money on me. But I'll get it, I'll ring someone.

Woman

do you still want the ambulance?

Dana

of course I want the ambulance. We have money in a bank. We have money. Lots of money. Fucking hell, demon, I'll take the money, please someone. Please someone just help my sister. Please please please. PLEASE.

SIXTEEN

Jasmine appears in a hospital gown.

Dana is waiting for her.

Jasmine starts to talk, serious and hard on herself.

Jasmine

I thought when it came to it, I would be good at it. I thought I would find it all instinctive. I thought maybe there would be this part of me that had been waiting all these years, that would know exactly what to do. But – hold on to it, that's the first thing isn't it? Rule number one. You want to be a mother, hold on to it. Seal it in, don't let it go all over the floor.

Dana

Jasmine –

Jasmine

that is kind of the first base, the easy slopes

Dana

listen to me

Jasmine

it's right that this happened.

Dana

no it isn't

Jasmine

I've got my head around it. I wasn't even sure that I
wanted it until today so it is fair enough.

Dana

come here –

Jasmine

I was stupid, see. If I had been one of the good
mothers, I would have told it I loved it. I would have
known it was precious. I would have put my knees
together, I would have taped myself up. Sat down
more. You should have made me do that. Why wasn't
I sitting? I could have stayed in bed. I shouldn't be here
with you, on this stupid trip, what was I thinking?
you have got to know how precious things are if you
want to hang on to them.

Dana

that isn't true

Jasmine

and if I was this stupid before, imagine how it could
have been after it was born? What if I still didn't
realise, and I then I forgot it and left it someplace?
Dana, what if I had gone on another jaunt with
you because I was dumb and left it someplace? And

then it got run over or stolen by wolves or kicked
about by ogres?
or what if I had picked it up wrong, because I still
didn't know, and I hurt its little neck? You know you
have to be careful of their little necks. What if I didn't
realise? What if I was listening to you going on and
not noticing what I was doing? What if the head fell
off? What if the neck snapped and the head fell off?
then I would have this headless baby, I would have
this horrible headless baby and what do you do with a
baby that doesn't have a head? I wouldn't have
known how to cuddle and comfort something like
that. I would get cross. I would shout at it because I
was so tired and it wouldn't feed. It would just bleed.
Bleed and bleed all over the floor. I would shake it. I
would hurt it, I would get very angry and shake it.
Stop bleeding I would say. Stop bleeding. You can't
bleed like this, you have to stop bleeding and live. You
have to live. You have to be my boy. You have to let
me put my arms around you and you have to grow up
and ask about the stars. You can't ask about the stars
if you are bleeding like this. You are just blood you
aren't a child. You put blood in a pot and make a
pudding. You mop it up with a sponge. You soak it up
with tissues and flush it down the loo. There is
nothing to you. You can't be my boy, my precious
bundle of child, you are just blood.
down the toilet you go. Blood.

Dana holds her.

Jasmine opens her mouth but can't make a sound.

SEVENTEEN

*Jasmine and Dana are by the roadside. They are in
tatters now.*

Dana is trying to hitch a lift.

The Librarian is with them but sitting a little way back.

Dana
I think it will get easier now.

Librarian
really?

Dana
yes
we have hit rock bottom.
let's face it, it can't be much worse than this.
we lost everything.
every single thing we had, we lost. Didn't we?
we even lost the suitcase that held everything we had.
whatever happens now, it can't be as bad.

Librarian
it's Monday

Dana
I know that

Librarian
I'm just saying that it is technically, it is Monday
lunchtime and you are nowhere near Alexandria

Beat.

Dana
maybe I can speak to them on the phone. You can
rearrange these things. When we tell them what has
happened to us on our journey they will understand.

Librarian
of course they will.

Beat.

you sold your phone to pay for Jasmine's treatment

Dana
I know I sold my phone
do you have to tell me everything that I already know?

Librarian
so how are you going to call?

Dana
I'll work it out

Librarian
there aren't many phone boxes that are working

Dana
I said I'll work it out

Librarian
and anyway you need a coin

Dana
thank you so much

Librarian
do you want a book to help you?

Dana
no thanks

Librarian
sure?

Dana
absolutely
no fucking books

Librarian
you have to go through lots of countries to get to
Alexandria, so anyway even if you do manage to
make a call –

Dana
we can go through lots of countries

Librarian

the borders are shut. Istanbul has shut its borders one
way, Alexandria the other
all of Europe is trying to get out

Dana

they'll let us through

Librarian

you think
why you?

Dana

I have a presentation to give. When I explain they will
let us through

Librarian

it's quite different over there. Better
of course, everyone wants to get through

Dana

well that means when we get there, things will be
easier
when we get there

Librarian

when you call them maybe you should ask them for
some kind of identification. Something that says they
invited you
I'm just thinking ahead

Dana

okay I'll ask them

Beat.

do you think there are going to be any cars coming by
this way? when did you last see a car?

Librarian

why do you want a car, you won't get a lift.

Dana
is there anything constructive you could say?

Librarian
Jasmine is anaemic.
she needs some iron.

Dana
I know that.

Beat.

Librarian
I'm just saying if you don't get her some help soon,
parts of her will start to fail –

Dana
could you look it up on a database, when did the last
car drive past on this particular piece of road?

Librarian
here?

Dana
yes

Librarian
alright

Dana
I saw people begging.
I saw a pile of people –

Librarian
I didn't see that

Dana
well, you were looking the wrong way
haven't you got a book about it?

Librarian
Extreme Poverty, yes. I believe I have

Dana
the sort where you have to sell your children?

Librarian
yes, there are various titles in that series

Dana
what are they called?

Librarian
there are lots of them, volumes and volumes
new ones coming out all the time. Do you want a new
release?

Dana
back there. There was a tiny little toddler they put out
to do the begging for them.

Librarian
that's probably a story told in an appendix somewhere

Dana
they didn't even do the begging themselves.

Librarian
common these days

Dana
I went up to the toddler and asked him where his
parents were, but they weren't there. They just left
him on the road

Librarian
maybe they had other things to do

Dana
what other things?
he was their toddler
what other things are there?

Librarian
I don't know.

I'm sure I have got a book about other things that
people might be doing

Dana
how could they have left him there. Right by the
roadside?

Librarian
don't ask me

Dana
that doesn't happen
no one does that.

Librarian
look around you.
do you recognise a single thing any more?

Dana looks around.

Dana
maybe it wasn't their toddler

Librarian
maybe.

Beat.

Dana
is there a guidebook to this place?

Librarian
there is a guidebook to every place.

Dana
what is it called here then?

Librarian
I don't think it has a name.

Dana
it's hell then
it might have been Europe yesterday.

I asked the man in the shop if he would give me some
water. I asked the woman by the tap. I just want some
water

Librarian

technically the water situation is complicated, and a
bit political

Dana

it's really fucking screwed, isn't it?
there was nothing in the shop because everyone had
gone crazy and grabbed it for themselves. The police
aren't being paid any more so they don't care. They
are doing most of the grabbing. You ask someone to
help you they will just knife you.

Beat.

people did use to care, didn't they? We didn't just
imagine it.

Librarian

they did use to, yes

Beat.

to cut a long story short. There's no petrol in the
pumps, of course there are no cars. I don't have a
book but a very nicely written article about it. With
photos. There is hardly any petrol in most of the old
eurozone countries so people have started to use a
bicycle.
the bicycle has made a resurgence
those that have one

Dana

where the fuck will I get a bicycle from?

Librarian

I am not saying you should get a bicycle, I am just
saying people are resilient. They use what they have

Dana
this is resilience?

Beat.

what am I going to do with her?

Librarian
I can't carry her. I've got all the books.
can she walk?

Dana
I don't know.

She sits down next to Jasmine.

were you asleep?

Jasmine
maybe a little

Dana
we need to try to get to the border. Then we can still
get to the presentation.
If I can do the presentation I can get the job. I can get
the job, I can get us out of this.

Jasmine
will they have a place where I can rest?

Dana
yes, I think that is exactly what they'll have

Jasmine
after the presentation?

Dana
exactly.

Jasmine
we don't have any money
don't you need money to get to the border?

Dana
I don't think so

Librarian
technically, you do

Dana
please shut up.

Jasmine
you do need money, Dana

Dana
alright, but don't worry about it, I'll get us some money. I'll get a short-term loan if necessary, we can pay it back when I get the job.

Jasmine
you can't get a loan

Dana
I'll get a loan
can you stand up?

Jasmine
when we see the doctor we could ask him to check the baby as well. Could we?

Dana
the baby?

Librarian
you didn't tell her?

Dana
I did tell her

Jasmine
do you think there are still doctors?

Dana
you lost the baby, love

Jasmine
no

Dana
Jasmine honey, you lost the baby.

Beat.

Jasmine
don't be silly, that's just a joke

Dana
no

Jasmine
no?

Dana
sorry.

Jasmine
oh yes. I lost the baby. I keep forgetting.
silly of me to forget something like that. Just when it
comes, when we have it in our arms?
we won't put it out to beg for us, would we?

Dana
but we won't

Jasmine
no, we won't

Beat.

Dana
I mean we wouldn't even if we could

Jasmine
what?

Dana
we haven't got the baby any more. The baby was just
blood

Jasmine
 are you sure?

Dana
 I'm sure

Jasmine
 you always say the meanest things. I don't know
 whether to believe you. Why won't we have it in our
 arms?

Dana
 Jasmine sweetheart –

Jasmine
 I know I know it's gone.
 you said it's gone. I just have to keep remembering.
 why can't I keep remembering?

Dana
 please stay strong

Jasmine
 I am strong

Dana
 I have to get you to the border

Librarian
 you need money to get to the border

Dana
 will you stop saying that –
 I know we haven't got money but we'll get some

Jasmine
 I don't even want to go to the border. I'm happy here,
 in the dust
 can't I just lie down here and forget about it all.

Dana
 I don't think you should do that.

Beat.

> Sit up. Sit up, Jaz
> you remember how you always looked after me, and
> you always had this strength whatever happened, you
> could be steady, and stable and –

Jasmine
> let me lie down –

Dana (*to the Librarian*)
> can you look after her?
> while I go and get some money

Librarian
> yes

Dana
> just make sure no one hurts her

Librarian
> you said you wouldn't

Dana
> I know what I said

Librarian
> he will have won

Dana
> he has won. He has reduced us to nothing. He won.
> look at us, he fucking won.
> will you look after her or not?

Librarian
> you'll need some books

Dana
> I don't need books

Librarian
> I think you should have them, there are things that are
> going to help you in these books

Dana
like what?

Librarian
taking your clothes off in front of a stranger

Dana
I've done that before

Librarian
The Economics of Selling Oneself

Dana
hardly

Librarian
How to Look Like You Are Enjoying Something while Your Skin Is Repelled

Dana
okay I'll take that.

Librarian
How to Stop Gagging with Someone's Putrid Penis in Your Mouth
I think you should take this one too.
How to Make Sure You Don't Get Strangled. How to Not Get a Disease that Will Kill You. How to Stay Alive during Prostitution.

She takes the books.

one final one, *How to Forget the Whole Thing Once It Is Over*

Dana
I won't forget the whole thing

Librarian
there are some really good books on self-meditation. Self-hypnosis. Letting everything go.

Dana
look after my beautiful sister Jasmine. Would you
please do that?

EIGHTEEN

*Dana lifts her clothes up, rips at them to make herself
look more alluring.*

*A man comes along. He throws a blanket and a horrible
old pillow on the floor.*

Dana tries to pin him down on price before they start.

Dana
my price is 45 euros.

Punter
you have to be kidding

Dana
45 euros and I'll give you a good time

Punter
have you done this before?

Dana
yes

Punter
only a line like that, people don't use it.

Dana
do you want to do this or not?

Punter
of course, but a 'good time', don't say that. And 45
euros, sorry to say, 45 euros and you get someone a
bit more –

Dana
what?

Punter
well-kept, don't want to be rude but
someone whose hair doesn't look like it is already
falling out.

Dana
25 then

Punter
15

Dana
that's too little, you don't know what I am giving you

Punter
I am pretty sure I do
I am pretty sure I know exactly.

Dana
I have a sister who isn't well, I have to get her out of
here

Punter
we all have to get out of here.
you think everyone isn't desperate to get out of this
place?
15 or nothing

Dana
17

Punter
sorry not interested

Dana
alright. 15

He laughs.

Punter
how about 10?

Dana
you just said 15

Punter
I like this, aren't you enjoying this bit?

Dana
devil, is this you?

Punter
what?

Dana
if this is a game –

Punter
I thought we were talking about a price

Dana
we are. Ten.

Punter
let's see what you've got then.

Dana starts to take off her clothes. She is embarrassed.

Dana
will you take off your clothes too?

Punter
eventually.

Dana
only I feel a bit –

Punter
you really aren't used to this, are you?

Beat.

Dana takes her shirt off.

Underneath the birthmark is all over her.

Punter
  what's wrong with you?

Dana
  nothing

Punter
  that mark all over you, what is it?

Dana
  it's just a birthmark
  I was born with it.

Punter
  never seen a birthmark like that before.

He comes towards her.

  does it hurt?

Dana
  no

Punter
  it's like a tattoo
  I like it.

Dana
  do you?

Punter
  what do you do?

Dana
  what do you want?

Punter
  I want everything. All ways.
  don't worry, when you see what I've got, you'll have
  a smile on your face

She kisses him.

  more

She starts to caress him through his clothes.

more

She unzips his trousers.

more

She takes his cock into her mouth.
He grabs her hair and pulls her back.
He pulls up her skirt, violent suddenly, and enters her.
The sex is brutal, almost rape.
It hurts her.
It hurts her more and more with every thrust.

Dana tries to stand up, she talks to the Interviewers.

Dana
for my presentation I wanted to speak about the customer experience. How the customer experience can affect the moment of money transfer. If the customer has been satisfied, then the handing over of money can prove more

She finds it difficult to continue.

it can prove more . . .

She is sore, she has been brutally treated.

if the encounter has been seen to be a good one then the customer –

She looks about her.

why won't you talk to me any more?
where are you? Devil, I know you are still there

The lights from the interview come on.

is that you?

Interviewer 1
Ms Edwards?

Dana
oh

Interviewer 2
can you hear us?

Dana
yes

Interviewer 1
we were expecting you last Monday.

Dana
I'm sorry about that

Interviewer 3
is that all you have to say?

Dana
I got held up

Interviewer 2
if we are to hold this research grant for you –

Dana
I'll be there

Interviewer 3
when, Ms Edwards?

Dana
as soon as I can.
can you help me get to the border?

Interviewer 2
we leave travel arrangements up to the individuals.
We understand that this is a difficult time for those
coming from the European Union, but

Dana

they have more or less closed the border into Turkey,
and if we go by boat –

Interviewer 3

we are sure you will find a way

Dana

there is no way.
all the borders are shut

Interviewer 1

we'll leave it open for a week.

Dana

could you give me a piece of paper saying that you
have invited me?

Interviewer 1

we aren't really sure

Interviewer 3

the administrative burden

Dana

if you could give me a piece of paper saying that I
have a position to go to

Interviewer 2

but you don't have a position. That is just the matter
that we are discussing.

Interviewer 3

you might have a position

Dana

there are thousands of people ahead of me
even if they reopen the borders

Interviewer 3

are you saying you want to cancel, Ms Edwards?

Beat.

Interviewer 1
there are plenty of others we could fill this post with.

Dana
no

Interviewer 2
you'll be here?

Dana
I'll be there

Interviewer 1
we'll see you soon then.

The voices seem to go. Dana is left alone in the space.

Dana
devil?

She stands in the bright light.

I can tell you are there.
you are everywhere now. I can feel you. Hear you.
you are in every face. Every carcass that was a person.
You are in the looters and the loan sharks. The
racketeers and the lost.
you might as well reveal yourself.
have your victory.
enjoy the last laugh

Beat.

you have had it all. What more is there?

Dana is still having sex with the Punter.

He comes to a noisy climax.

Thank god it is over.

The man zips his trousers back up.

He gets some money out of his wallet, that he carefully puts on the ground next to her.

Punter
thank you. That was nice.

Then he goes.

Dana is left alone.

Dana
oh god.

She is bruised and broken.

She just about manages to sit up.

She cries out once or twice. He really hurt her.

She gathers up the money.

A woman comes along. She is wearing tattered clothes that perhaps once looked smart.

Marta
hello?

Dana
hello.

Marta
you look hurt, are you okay?

Dana
not really

There is a second woman behind her. She is also covered in dirt.

Clara
what's up with her?

Marta
I'm not sure

Dana
I'll be alright

Marta
you look bruised

Clara
only this is kind of where we are

Dana
what?

Clara
this whole park

Marta
give her a minute

Clara
why?

Marta
she's hurt

Clara
we're all hurt
aren't you hurt? Fuck, who isn't hurt?

Dana
I'm sorry I didn't realise

Marta
it isn't marked out

Dana
I thought it was just a park

Clara
far as those trees, back to the path. Ours. Past the
swings down to the road

Dana
okay

Clara

if you want the bit behind the car park you have to
fight one of the girls over there for it, good luck to you

Dana

I don't want to fight.

Marta

they used to be primary school teachers but you
wouldn't know it now

Dana

I'm going

Clara

how much did you make out of interest?

Marta

let her go

Clara

I'm just asking

Dana

not much really

Dana picks up her bits and pieces and starts to move

Clara

go on let us look
we know how it works, we can help you
see if you could get more next time

Dana

there won't be a next time

Clara

let me see

Dana isn't sure whether to trust them.

Marta

we know what this is like
we're the same as you

She shows them, her hand still shaking.

Marta
 not bad
 horrible isn't it?

Clara
 it doesn't matter how it is –

Marta
 don't be brutal

Clara
 she has to understand, we've got nothing else, only
 this place and ourselves

Dana
 what?

Marta
 she used to be a lawyer

Clara
 it's about fairness

Dana
 I told you, I didn't know this place was yours

Clara
 thing is, you can't not know things any more. You
 can't stumble.

Dana
 I'm going

Marta
 if we had any choice

Clara
 it's a jungle now, the girls over there, the ones that way

Dana
 my sister has just lost a baby, and she needs to be
 treated

Clara

she needs, you need. Who is talking about need
anyway? It's a useless term. Everyone needs
I've got a mother who's dying, she's got three daughters

Marta

hand it over, make it easy

Dana

I know you

Marta

don't be stupid

Dana

you used to be on the telly –
you used to read the news

Marta

hey – there's no problem here

Dana

what happened to you?

Clara takes the money. She passes it to Marta.

Clara

you want to save your sister? Grow some teeth

Dana

what did you say?

Dana finds the strength of a warrior.

She rushes at Clara, savage for a second.

Clara

oi

Clara is savage back.

give that here –

Dana

it's mine

Marta is savage too.

Dana
fuck you, I earned it

Marta
does it matter?

Dana attacks them. She gets the money back.

They turn on her.

They are more brutal and there are two of them.

Marta speaks aloud as she thumps her.

Marta
this is not personal. We told you. We need it, that's all.

Dana loses and is kicked repeatedly.

The women take her money.

They kick her again, just to make sure.

Dana is left beaten up like a piece of meat.

Clara
it's okay, she's got a fanny hasn't she? She can use it
again.

NINETEEN

The boat.

*Jasmine and Dana are on a boat. With them on the boat
are hundreds of other people. They are jammed in like
sardines.*

Jasmine
do you think we should ring our local politician?

Dana
what?

Jasmine

    well, someone must still be trying to make things a bit
    better

Dana

    I don't think the politicians are still working

Jasmine

    of course they are
    they always say on the telly you can ring them
    only there are so many people we have to ring them
    before everyone else does, everybody is grabbing, you
    get there first

Dana

    where?

Jasmine

    to the telephone.
    ooh god

Dana

    it's alright, just a wave

Jasmine

    the politicians will be getting aid from other countries,
    we can tell them how to spend it, they will thank us
    probably

Dana

    what aid?

Jasmine

    from all those countries that we used to give aid to.
    African countries

Dana

    we gave a bit to
    we didn't give very much

Jasmine

    it's their turn to help us now, they can't just watch
    was that another wave?

Dana
  yes I think so

Jasmine
  do I even like boats?

Dana
  try to like them

Jasmine
  there should be a roof. Tell the politician that when
  you get to the phone. A boat with this number of
  people –
  they said they would only take eighty, this must be
  over three hundred

Dana
  they do this run every night, it'll be fine

Jasmine
  oh god

Dana
  another wave, a bit of swell

Jasmine
  they should sail in the day, if you could see the waves
  coming you could get ready for them

Dana
  I think it has to be at night
  so no one sees

Jasmine
  did we have to pay for this?

Dana
  don't worry about the money

Jasmine
  I do worry about the money.

Beat.

it's an outrage, this should be a free service. People
like us need to be saved. And crammed in like this.
Treated like sardines.
it hasn't even got seats for us all
we would need a seat for the baby if we still had it.
Tell the politician that, there aren't even baby seats.
Don't worry, I am remembering that we lost the baby,
but even still –

Dana
I guess it is what makes it worth their while. They are
taking a risk after all

Jasmine
we are taking a risk
this boat should have been rebuilt years ago
maybe we should try and get near an edge, then if
anything happens we can try and grab one of the life
rings.

Dana
we can't move
I don't think we should try and move now

Jasmine
did you say if I liked boats?

Dana
I said you loved them

Jasmine
I feel quite sick

Dana
you'll be fine
hang on to my hand.

Jasmine hangs on to Dana's hand.

Jasmine
if the baby was here we would have to hang on to it

very tight. make sure it didn't go near the edge. This
would be a terrible journey with a baby

Dana
you remember that we lost the baby?

Jasmine
of course I do.
I was just telling the baby we lost it. It's a naughty
baby, keeps forgetting.
there is nothing wrong with me

Dana
I know

Jasmine
will they be glad to see us when we get to Alexandria?

Dana
maybe

Jasmine
I hope so. All this way.
I want a clean bed with clean sheets

Dana
granted

Jasmine
a house with a back yard, maybe a swing

Dana
okay

Jasmine
fresh water out of a tap, bread
just like at home
shoes that don't make my feet bleed

Dana
once I get the job, it will all be sorted

Jasmine
we won't ever be going back home, will we?

Dana
I don't think there is anything left for us there.

Beat.

Jasmine
I don't like the idea of not existing.
of being a person but not a person. Like the baby

Dana
the baby –

Jasmine
is dead I know, whereas we –
we'll just be illegal. I understand.

Dana
when we get there, it will get better.
it will all feel better

There is a sudden jolt.

Jasmine
what was that?

Dana
what?

Jasmine
that bump

Dana
we're out on the open sea, there are bound to be some
bumps

Jasmine
I wish I could swim

Dana
if anything goes wrong, you grab a life ring

Jasmine

what about the baby?

Dana

we don't have the baby remember

Jasmine

oh yes, I forgot again. Silly baby made me forget.
they're greedy the people who run this ship. There's
no cover, not enough life-jackets, nowhere to sit

Dana

it doesn't matter how we get there, we just get there
okay?

Jasmine

okay.

The Librarian comes and taps Dana on the shoulder.

Dana

not now

Librarian

you'll need a book

Dana

I don't want a book
I am getting out of this. When we are there

Librarian

Rough Crossings for the Weak in Spirit

Dana

we aren't weak in spirit
I need to hold my sister's hand

Librarian

okay, *How to Spot Danger and Do Something About It*

Dana

we aren't in danger
the sea is alright, it's a short crossing, we go via Crete

Librarian

How to Spot Rocks in the Dark

Dana

there aren't any rocks

Librarian

How to Spot Rocks You Can't See, though technically
this is a guide to navigational techniques and this boat
doesn't have any, so –

Dana

this boat doesn't have any?

Librarian

they have a compass and some other stuff
I might have a book on that.
oh, people are puking, do you want something on
how to stop getting covered in vomit in an open-aired
vessel?

Dana

not really.

Librarian

okay.
How to Hold Your Breath for a Very Long Time

Dana

I don't need to hold my breath, why would I need to
hold my breath?

Librarian

you need to hold your breath for a very long time,
Dana

Dana

I am out in the air, I don't need to hold my breath
see, I am breathing

Librarian

hold your breath now, Dana
hold your breath for a very long time

HOW TO HOLD YOUR BREATH

The interview lights come back on.

Dana is drenched, and standing there sopping wet.

Interviewer 1
Ms Edwards

Dana
yes

Interviewer 1
you seem not to be breathing.

Dana
I am breathing.
I'm holding my breath

Interviewer 1
you seem to be going under

Dana
I'm not going under

Interviewer 2
if this means you can't give your presentation, this
will cause us no end of headache

Dana
I'll give my presentation

Interviewer 2
you seem to be still, Ms Edwards

Dana
I'm not still

Interviewer 1
you seem to be being pulled under, there are others
screaming but you don't seem to be one of them

Dana
I'm screaming but it's hard when you are holding your
breath

Interviewer 1
no words are coming.

Interviewer 3
Ms Edwards

Dana
I'm holding my breath, how can words be coming out
of my mouth

Interviewer 2
you needed to hold your breath earlier

Dana
I'm holding it now

Interviewer 1
the water as you hit it caused you shock

Interviewer 3
you got swept away, you hit your head

Dana
no that is not right
I'm holding my breath
I'm holding my breath
I'm holding my breath.

TWENTY

The demon is behind Dana.

He picks her up and carries her like a small child.

She is inert.

And soaking wet. Hair bedraggled.

He is dressed in uniform. He works for the UN.

*As he carries her forward a trolley is brought. A rough-
and-ready hospital is created.*

The demon puts Dana on the hospital trolley.

A female Doctor comes and checks her over.

Jarron
　she was a migrant

Doctor
　we don't have her name?

Jarron
　I don't think so, no

Doctor
　well I doubt anyone will bother with dental records.
　We'll just put 'unknown woman' on the death
　certificate. Cause of death?

Jarron
　drowning and hypothermic shock
　the electrolytes in her blood

Doctor
　she held her breath for too long.

Jarron
　basically
　the trauma to the head might have killed her first
　if she was lucky

The Doctor looks her over.

Doctor
　well, if you will be stupid enough to cross on a boat
　like that
　they bring it on themselves
　what is this mark on her?

Jarron
　I think it was the lack of oxygen as she went down

Doctor
　strange, I haven't seen one like that before. How
　many have we got?

Jarron

this is the ninety-third, but they are still pulling them out of the water

Doctor

why do they do it?
why do they take the risk?

Beat.

Jarron

what should we do with the body?

Doctor

we'll organise some kind of burial. See, that is our problem too. We either bury them here or pay to have them shipped back to where they came from. Either way it comes to us to fork out. The economics of the European collapse will go on and on.

The Doctor starts to go off.

get her processed and get on to the other ones. Don't spend too long

The devil sits beside Dana.

He puts his hand on her cheek.

He touches her gently across her body.

He lifts her up and sits behind her.

He cradles her.

The Librarian comes in.

Jarron

what are you doing?

Librarian

what are you doing?

The devil doesn't have an answer to that.

Librarian
I was just delivering some books

Jarron
I don't think she needs books now

Librarian
on the contrary, she needs lots of books.
where she is going, it gets even more complicated.

Jarron
you weren't a good guide
look what happened to her

Librarian
you did this, not me

Jarron
I didn't do a single thing

Librarian
alright, but you watched. You didn't stop it.

Jarron
she was naive. She had to see a thing or two

Beat.

shall I wake her?

Beat.

do you want me to wake her?

Librarian
you can't wake her
technically she is dead

Jarron
technically, her heart is still beating. Faintly but it's
present. She could go either way in truth.
on the one hand, a shot of adrenaline and eyes open.
Some oxygen perhaps if she needs it. On the other,

just leave her on a trolley and it will be over in an
hour or so.

The demon takes a small syringe out of his pocket.

I have it right here
the two gates

Librarian
don't wake her

Jarron
why not?

Librarian
her sister also died.
I just think one without the other
she has been through enough, this little body

Jarron
she deserved it. She thought she could make me love
her, how wrong she was.

He lifts the ampule of adrenaline.

The Librarian stops him.

you are only supposed to advise, you aren't supposed
to do anything. You are the librarian, you stay in your
corner

Librarian
even the corner man can stand up

Jarron
oh can he?

Librarian
she has been through enough, I said let it stop

The demon deliberates.

Jarron
 and let her go?

Librarian
 she's got nothing left, after all, has she? You proved
 your point

Jarron
 she has got everything. What do you mean, nothing?
 she made it over the crossing. She made it to this side.
 We could wake her up. Give her some clothes. She
 could do her presentation, get the job, decent salary,
 buy a flat
 she is one of the lucky ones
 she could have everything
 how can you say she has got nothing?

Librarian
 but her eyes are open now, as you said, she can't shut
 them again. Even you can't shut them. What she has
 seen – she thought that men and women were
 basically good, human nature in essence benign. Then
 she saw it wash all away, one crisis and the jungle
 came at her, she heard the hyenas howling, saw hell
 etched on other people's faces. Let's face it, she saw
 the dark swamp at the bottom of the human soul and
 once you have seen that –

Jarron
 we make her forget then.
 easy
 we make her forget.
 we put her in a trance, we wash it off. She is as good
 as dead, we wash her in the river between the two
 worlds if we have to.

The devil starts to take off Dana's soaked clothes.

Librarian
 how can you forget all that?

393

Jarron
you can forget anything
stop making so much of it, so people get a bit nasty,
people like Dana they live in a hazy afternoon.
Pleasant but fragile, one slip through a crack –
if you dance on the cracks, after all, one day you'll fall
through, that has to be a saying. Has someone
important said that?
pass me those shoes, those shoes will suit her

The Librarian passes the shoes.

and a jacket I have laid over that chair

The Librarian passes the jacket.

He starts to put new clothes on her.

Modern clothes, clothes that she will look good in.

I'm going to wake her
you haven't been a good guide.
I am going to wake her.
find her a book

Librarian
like what?

Jarron
a book on modern living. A book that might have
'modern living' in the title. I don't know. *How to
Furnish a Flat in a Weekend? What to Wear when
You Want to Look Good. The Cinema Guide.* A
cookery book. A manual on which over-expensive car
to buy. *How to Get a Good Seat at the Theatre.
Which Charity You Should Give to to Make you Feel
Better. What to Say on a First Date. Topiary for
Beginners, The Low-Carb Diet, How to Write a
Novel, To Floss or Not to Floss.*
do you want me to go on?

He pulls Dana's hair back.

What Not to Wear, Social Media, Twitter, Pastry-
Making for Chefs, Meditation for People who Do Too
Much, The Work–Life Balance and How to Survive It

He washes her face.

To Smack or Not to Smack, History for Idiots, A
Guide to Alsace Wine, Beating Anxiety, Overcoming
Insomnia, Sinusitis, The Prostate Conundrum, How
to Chose a Wig, A Thousand Things to See before
You Die

*He gets her to stand up. Her eyes are still shut. But she
stands by herself.*

Jarron
Dana
Dana

*The voices of the interview panel join in with the calling
of her name.*

Dana.
Dana.
Dana.

The interview lights come on.

*Dana is standing there, now fully restored in smart
clothes suitable for an interview.*

Dana wakes with a sharp intake of breath.

Interviewer 1
if you would like to start your presentation now.

The curtain falls.

MEET ME AT DAWN

Meet Me at Dawn was first performed at the Traverse Theatre, Edinburgh, on 6 August 2017. The cast was as follows:

Helen Sharon Duncan-Brewster
Robyn Neve McIntosh

Director Orla O'Loughlin
Designer Fred Meller
Lighting Designer Simon Wilkinson
Composer & Sound Designer Danny Krass
Assistant Director Fiona Mackinnon
Movement Advisers White & Givan
Voice Coach Ros Steen

Characters

Robyn

Helen

The play is set on a beach

Note on Punctuation

The spoken lines in this text start with a lower-case letter to stop each line reading like a statement; lines are often incomplete phrases, half-thoughts or utterances that pass from one to another, and are rarely whole sentences.

In general the spoken text is laid out according to each character's process of reasoning with each new line indicating a new thought.

A woman in her forties, Robyn, speaks to the audience.

Robyn
it seems to me, and I know nothing – I know less than
nothing so anything I say you have to ignore really or
pretty much pretty much anyway but it seems to me –
in a time like this – in a place like this – that there is
the first bit, that's to say the bit that comes now, the
bit that comes before the rest but after the others, not
the first bit then but the bit that is now
and that bit is about asking a question
and the questions is

are you okay?

Helen
jesus

Robyn
are you okay?

Beat.

Helen, Helen, are you okay?

Helen
yes I think

Robyn
bloody hell –

Helen
yes I think

Robyn
you're okay?

Helen
yes

Helen comes on to stage.

She is soaking wet.

Helen
yes
fucking hell, yes I think

Robyn
I know

Helen
shit

Robyn
I know
I know

Helen
I thought we were –

Robyn
we were

Helen
I mean I really thought –

Robyn
me too

Helen
fuck
yes I'm alright
are you?

The two women are both soaked through.

They look at themselves. There is a sort of giddy hysteria.

Robyn
yes I think

Helen
both fine?

Robyn
both fine

Helen
because I couldn't really –

Robyn
no, no –

Helen
I mean out there, in that place –

Robyn
I understand

Helen
every man for himself, or every woman –
I was, there was a sort of cloud over my thinking
and I couldn't, and I know I should have –
I know I should have, you were there of course I knew
you were struggling but –

Robyn
I was the same

They look at each other.

I was the same, it's okay

Helen
I would have helped you if I could

Robyn
me too. I said it's okay

Helen

    I would've swum back in for you
    I would've done anything for you
    it was just that –

Robyn

    I get it

Beat.

    but look
    we're both okay
    does it matter? We're both okay

Helen looks at herself. Her arms and legs.

She laughs a bit.

Helen

    yeah

She kind of whoops.

    yes yes

She whoops again.

    I'm kind of buzzing in fact, like my heart is going
    like it's going to come out of my ears or something
    do you think my heart might actually?

Robyn

    I doubt it

Helen

    like it's pumping louder or stronger or
    you could bottle this, you could actually sell this
    this this feeling
    like the strongest coffee or

Robyn

    I'm not sure I like it

Helen

    use it though? if we could keep this –
    imagine if you could access this when you –
    okay so you don't like it but imagine if you could

Robyn

    I thought we were properly

Helen

    but imagine if you could train yourself, in a meeting
    or
    I can fucking rule the world
    we could fucking rule the world
    couldn't we?
    if you could bring this up to order

Robyn

    I thought we were –

Helen

    hands feet
    march or lift, lift a car or a house or
    you know those stories, people lift houses off children
    or
    and now we know we are –
    we can, this is in us too
    all I am saying is
    it's changed, we've changed, there's this
    well it's amazing isn't it? We are going to forget this
    we shouldn't forget this
    we should train this into our muscle memory

Robyn

    I think I'm actually going to be sick

Helen

    oh

Beat.

Robyn
sorry I know you are all – but
I feel dreadful

Beat.

Helen
I'll find you something to vomit in

Robyn
on the shore?

They look around.

Helen
well what do you want?

Robyn
I want to feel better
I want not to be wet
I want not to be shivering
I want that not to have happened
I want to be home
with you

Helen
maybe you should take your clothes off
some of them
get your shoes off anyway
that jumper, it's holding the water
probably keeping you colder

Robyn
aren't you cold?

Helen
I'm like a furnace
yes alright cold a bit
but mainly – fucking hell

Robyn
  it will hit you in a minute
  you're probably even colder than me but the shock

Helen
  I feel fine
  I feel great
  I feel – I am sorry that you don't feel all that good but

Robyn
  I feel like vomiting is that alright?
  I mean I don't want to spoil what you have got with
  this great fucking feeling

Beat.

  sorry

Helen comes over.

Helen
  no, I'm a moron

Robyn
  I really think I'm going to vomit, I'm not mucking
  about

Helen
  I know

Robyn
  don't rub my back

Helen
  I wasn't going to

Beat.

  it's the salt water isn't it?

Robyn
  you're the scientist

Helen
> salt water always makes you feel sick
> if you swallowed some of that then –

Robyn retches.

She retches again.

Helen stands there looking spare.

Robyn
> and don't watch me either
> it's horrible to watch someone being sick

Helen
> what am I supposed to do?

Robyn
> find the way back to the car

Helen
> can you walk?

Robyn
> my feet aren't vomiting are they it's just my –
> oh god

She retches again.

Helen looks around.

Helen
> what do we do about the boat do you think?

Beat.

> sorry, concentrate on –
> you just

Helen looks over, out into the water.

> it's just we'll have to tell them won't we?

Robyn
> do we really have to talk about this now?

Helen

no, sure
just we should tell them?
shouldn't we? get the money back,
damn thing wasn't seaworthy, might get a fat lot of
compensation
the thing was too expensive anyway, I said that
didn't –

Robyn

why did you say that word?

Helen

what word?

Robyn

compensation?

Helen

they hired us a boat that sank, don't be stupid
we should at least get our money back
they probably saw anyway, they were probably
laughing
two women like us, out in a boat?
I bet it looked hilarious

Robyn

they won't have meant it

Helen

of course they won't
but I bet it looked –
I bet it looked –
that is all I am saying, I bet it looked –
well we aren't made for –

Beat.

Silence for a second.

They look at each other.

Robyn
you talk too much

Helen
you love me

Robyn
you drive me crazy

Helen
crazy in a good way?

Robyn
not always

Helen
but sometimes?

Robyn
sometimes, yes

Helen looks about..

Helen
there you go you see, sometimes,
sometimes sometimes, that is good enough
I drive you crazy, sometimes. What a fucking love
poem
you ready to walk back to the car?

Robyn
I suppose

Helen
what's that?

Robyn
where?

Helen
you have something on you

Robyn
oh

Helen
    there on your –
    hang on

She sees something on Robyn's cardigan.

Helen
    nothing
    just a –

Robyn
    well what?

Helen
    just a, I don't know, an insect
    just a, some kind of moth

Robyn
    let me see

Helen
    it's like it's got tangled in your, wait a sec

She gets it off.

    here

They look at it.

Robyn
    poor fucker

Helen
    pretty though

Robyn takes it.

Robyn
    shouldn't even be here
    should be inland
    you don't get moths by the sea

Helen
    I don't know

Robyn
you're the scientist

Helen
I study rocks, not living things

Robyn
it's a dead one

Helen
even still

Robyn holds it in her hand.

Robyn
what should I do with it?

Helen
put it down

Robyn
it's got beautiful red spots, one on each wing

Helen
what is wrong with you?
put it down yes

Robyn
maybe it flew on to me on the boat
maybe it was with me during all that
but then why isn't it wet?

She looks at it.

Helen
there is no meaning, there is no point trying to find
meaning
there is none. We had a horrible accident, a near miss.
It's a dead moth

Robyn
how romantic you are

Helen
    always
    my love poem back to you. It's a dead moth, pretty,
    yes, but a bit disgusting. Put it down

Robyn puts it down on the sand.

Robyn
    something will eat it

Helen
    yes

Robyn
    red spots and all
    vomit it back up for its babies

Helen
    almost certainly
    nature

Robyn
    I guess

Helen
    which way is the car?

Robyn
    I thought you would know

Helen
    not for certain

They both look around.

Robyn comes over.

    not at all actually

Robyn
    it was further back that boat place, it must be –

Helen
this isn't where we set off, is it?
or is that . . .

Robyn
not exactly no but
we're not even near

Helen looks around too.

Helen
we're further down the shore then
must be, we must have –

Robyn
alright but which way from here?

Helen
there was a path
there was a bridge
a tree – you said if we went swimming later we could
hang our clothes on it

Robyn looks about.

Robyn
no trees here

Helen
well if we walk further around –

Robyn
no bridge

Helen stands up.

Helen
have you got your phone?

Robyn
of course not
everything went down with the boat

They look around again.

which is precisely because the second question, after
the first the first being after the physical, is the
physical okay? Then comes where are we, the *where*
being not just geographically though that of course –
the *where* being something has changed that changed us
are we as we were before and somewhere in the dim
recesses of something –
somewhere in the dim is there a parallel us, and where
are they
is there a parallel you?
is there a parallel me? did something split there?
did we?
she said muscle memory and the muscle memory, is
the muscle memory of a place here or somewhere
else or –
so the question is –

Helen
where the fuck actually are we?

They look at each other. They look around.

where the fuck actually are we?

They look again.

where the fuck?

Robyn
I heard you

Helen
you didn't answer

Robyn
take your fucking jumper off, you're getting hysterical

Helen
where the hell are we?

Robyn
I don't know
what do you want, all the answers from me?
I don't know okay. I don't know
I'm as lost as you

They look again.

we went out in a boat
we got into trouble in the water

Robyn
we swam we –

Helen
this isn't where we left from

Robyn
okay so in our sort of muddle –
while we were sinking
we swam in an odd direction

Helen
maybe this is an island
maybe we landed on an island

Robyn
what kind of island is there?

Helen
I don't know

Robyn
really?

Helen
it's just a suggestion, just an idea about how come –
you go up there, you can see the shoreline snakes
around

does it snake around?
this might even be a tiny island but
we have no phone

Beat.

Robyn
it doesn't really matter what size of island it is
we don't even know if it is an island –

Helen
of course not but –

Robyn
we have no phone, that's the point. We're on a bit of
land, we don't know where we are, we are cold or
likely to get cold and we have no phone

Helen goes and looks at the bit of shoreline.

Helen
maybe we got carried down by the tide or something
and this is just –

Robyn
what?

Helen
we walk in one direction as far as we can, see if it
takes us back to here

Robyn
okay
or

Helen
you have a better idea?

Robyn
we wait I suppose

Helen
we wait here?

Robyn
we find out what here is

Helen
you can see the shore, over there
that must be the shore we came from, this is a kind of
–

Robyn
you can hardly see it

Helen
you can see *something* is there
you can see that something is there
Robyn – fuck's sake look
there is *something* there

Robyn
if you say so

Helen
maybe this is just a sandbank

Robyn
maybe it disappears at high tide you mean?

Helen
don't say that, no I didn't mean –

Robyn
we need to walk, we need to find out what it is

Helen
you can't fucking say there isn't anything there

Robyn
calm down

Helen
well look

Robyn
alright

there is *something* there
yes, there is where we came from but it doesn't do us
any bloody good does it?

Helen
the sun is out

Robyn
and that means?

Helen
that means we aren't going to die of hypothermia

Robyn
while we are waiting to be drowned at high tide

Helen
we are going to warm up
we might have to swim back, when we are ready

Robyn
I can't swim back, you can't swim back

Helen
we might have to do all kinds of things we didn't
realise we would which is why it is lucky we have all
this energy and power that we didn't think we could
ever possess

Robyn
only I don't
I feel sick

Helen
will you try Robyn please at least try

Beat.

Robyn
we could die of thirst

Helen
great trying

Robyn

well we could couldn't we?
you can't drink the sea

Helen

we're only going to be here for a few hours

Robyn

you hope

Helen

someone – the people who own the boat
the people who own the boat are going to say,
shouldn't they be back in by now?
they're going to look at their watches and go
they should be back
those women who took the boat out and who we
laughed at because we all knew they didn't know
what they were doing, you know those women

Robyn

you said they were con men

Helen

they're going to want to know what happened to their
boat, aren't they?
their boat is worth something, or they think it is
it went out with us on it
they're going to say what happened to those women,
at some stage
please try to be positive Robyn
the minute they've had that thought, we are okay
they will phone someone, they will pick up a phone
coastal rescue or something
someone will arrive in a speedboat with silver
blankets
they'll be thermoses and people and we'll be okay

Robyn looks out to the shore.

Robyn
I can't really see it

Helen
why does that not surprise me?
bloody hell, it's there
there

Robyn peers.

you need your eyes tested

She peers again.

I've told you that before.

Robyn
there's a kind of smudge

Helen
that's where we came from, this, that is –

Robyn
it's a cloud

Helen
no it's a place it's a place where we have our car, and
our home and our jobs and our bread that is
mouldering in the bread bin and the bins that need
emptying and a bed that needs clean sheets but is
really fucking fantastic to sleep on
and pillows and towels in the bathroom
and the dog that belongs to our neighbour but is
somehow ours
and all the dirt on the kitchen floor and the crap we
live with
that's where it all happens

Robyn
maybe there is water here anyway –
all this worry about being here

Helen

I'm not worried

Robyn

all this worry I have
and there could be a stream just there

Helen

are you actually thirsty or are you –

Robyn

I am actually thirsty

Beat.

Helen

okay so I will find some water
there really isn't much need for water since we will be
here a really short time but
you can survive days without water you realise that
and I'm pretty sure you had water at breakfast, but
yes if you need water
maybe we should write 'help us' or something in the
sand
and then –

Beat.

They look at each other.

Then a pause.

Robyn

what are you doing?

Helen

what do you mean?

Robyn

you've stopped talking

Helen

I'm thinking

Robyn
  you always talk

Beat.

Helen
  I am thinking okay
  is it not okay for me to think?

They both take a second to think.

  I'm thinking
  I'm still thinking

Pause.

It dawns on them that they are a bit fucked.

Robyn
  there's actually a person

Helen
  where?

Robyn
  I think that is someone

Helen
  can't see

Robyn
  over there
  look

Helen
  it's a smudge

Robyn
  a man I think or perhaps a woman

Helen
  you said there was a smudge, that's a smudge if ever
  I saw one

They both look.

    oh perhaps yes a woman

Robyn
    thank you

Helen
    and thank fuck

Robyn
    why did you say that?
    we don't know what kind of woman it is
    it could be a weird woman, she could be –

Helen
    does it matter if they are weird?
    a person will have a phone, man or woman I don't care, another person
    it doesn't matter who it is, if there is a person there is a phone
    isn't that right? Coastal rescue, they can ring the coastal rescue
    in today's world, every person who isn't a baby I suppose, I suppose not a baby but any person has a phone –

Robyn
    I don't have a phone
    she says
    the woman that we find

    and is it just me or is there something –
    is there something about the way the skin fits on her face or perhaps her eyebrows or –

    I don't have a phone she says again

    this is my precious Helen and this is a day and somehow we are here and you, you have to have a phone
    and I know I am muddled I know I am but –

Helen
what do you mean you don't have a phone?

Robyn
I don't have a phone, she says the same thing over and
over

Helen
but that can't be –

Robyn
maybe she lives without a phone, people do Helen,
people do live without a phone

Helen
out here?
surrounded by sea

Robyn
all I'm saying –

Helen
okay
okay, that's fine, no phone
you don't have a phone
how does one get off here? this place, how do you get
off it?

Pause.

Robyn
she doesn't say anything – the woman

Helen
sorry, just do you know how to get back to the
mainland?
is there a causeway, does the tide go out?

Robyn
I don't have a phone she says

Helen
why does she keep saying that?

Robyn

I don't have a phone
I don't have a phone

Helen

she's going on and on

Robyn

you're being rude

Helen

okay. Yes I see, we know you don't have a phone but
do you know about the tide?
I asked about the tide
I didn't actually ask you about your phone

Robyn

you did ask that

Helen

before yes
now I am asking, how does one get off this island?

Beat.

Robyn

she looks from me to Helen and back to me.

Helen

would you be able to help us?
we are trying to get off here?

Robyn

she says nothing

Helen

is it even an island, can you confirm this is an island?
perhaps it isn't an island, perhaps you –

Beat.

how do you live here?

Robyn
she looks pretty cold and –

Helen
how can you live here?

Beat.

Robyn
maybe you're talking too fast, you're always talking
too fast

Helen
it's not too fast –

Robyn
I don't think she is following –

Helen
of course she is following, she understood the first
question
sorry but

Pause.

we have a dog, we are looking after it for our
neighbour, we have to get back for our dog. even if
not for ourselves, the dog is left inside the house and
we have to get off this island

Robyn
maybe you are standing too close, there's something
obviously a bit . . .

Helen
what?

Robyn
maybe you are crowding her

Helen
you try

Robyn
hi

only we've been caught in a

Helen
only we've been caught in a

she repeats you

Robyn
I can hear that she repeats me
aha I see, yes but

Helen
aha I see, yes but

Robyn
okay

Helen
okay

Robyn
okay yes I get it
you are copying

Helen
you are copying

Beat.

Robyn moves further away.

Robyn
she's crazy

Helen
I think we established that

Robyn
but she obviously isn't drowned, I mean the fact that
she is here means on this whatever it is, that the tide

clearly doesn't come in and sweep her away every
night

Helen
well that's true

Robyn
something catches my eye

Helen
she's got your moth

Robyn
I can see that

Helen
she's picked it up

Robyn
it's not my moth, it doesn't matter if she has my moth
does it

Helen
what happened to it?
what happened to it?

Robyn
it had nothing to do with us
I promise
is that the answer? Is that what she is looking for

and the parallel thing, the parallel thing and the
moth –
there is something in muscle memory about the moth
the moth that should be wet but isn't
when she picks it up, I think I have seen this woman
and this moth
I have seen the moth but not here
I have not been here before
but I have seen that moth
the women buries it slightly

then brushes her hands
she starts to walk away
now wait a minute
please don't just walk away, please as you are here
and we are obviously in trouble –
tell us
how do you get off here? we really need some help
we seem to be trapped and as you are the only person
but she goes

Beat.

Helen

she knows every damn thing we are saying
she knows every little thing
she is doing this deliberately
she is winding us up
have you ever met a woman like that, prepared to
wind you up?

Robyn

she is unhinged in some way

Helen

of course she's unhinged
but that doesn't excuse it

Robyn

there is a parallel day
there is a parallel moth
I am sure there is a parallel moth
I have seen this moth before. This dry dead moth
it has two red spots. Helen is the person that is more
likely to know about what it is for, but for some
reason Helen isn't part of this. This moment
I don't know why Helen isn't but –
I just look at the colour.
there is a thing – what am I reaching for, before the
questions about who and where

was there . . .
there was a moth one day – which day – a moth that
one day I found and
someone said something
someone said, yes
someone said
someone said
no, someone said –
if I could just say what someone said . . . .
someone said
if I could remember what someone said

Beat.

someone said
I had the moth in my hand, I was looking at the moth
just bear with me, someone said
someone said something
someone said something
they said something
something terrible
and I felt that sick
just like I felt now
someone said something terrible and I felt that sick

Helen
I'm not saying we shouldn't forget her I think we
should stay as far away as possible but
if she knew she was winding us up
okay so we are on an island with a crazy woman but
it doesn't matter because she doesn't look dangerous,
though what would we know

Robyn
I feel really weird about this

Helen
what sort of weird?

Robyn
creeped out

Helen
don't be creeped out

Robyn
it's not just her though is it, it's being here stuck –
I feel a sort of claustrophobic
like when you are locked in somewhere and can't get
open the door

Helen
we won't be stuck for long

Robyn
we've no idea
we could be stuck for a week, the clouds are so low
you can't even see where the shore is

Helen
I can

Robyn
it's a smudge

Helen
I don't know what you are talking about then, I don't
know why you do this, yes it's not great, yes it's not
even all that okay but what can we do, what is the
point? you are almost dry now aren't you
we'll get back to the neighbour's dog
that is what you have to think, we will get back to
her, that dog and our lives
this is shit and the day went tits up but

Robyn
there is a muscle thing
there is a muscle thing going on

Helen
please Robyn

Robyn
and you saw the moth first and

Helen
what are you talking about?

Robyn
I don't know Helen
I don't know but I am in my kitchen

Helen
our kitchen

Robyn
alright our kitchen only
fuck my head, my head is doing something weird

Helen
you are concussed maybe

Robyn
I am standing in our kitchen yes
our kitchen or maybe my kitchen
I am standing at the sink
our sink fine, our sink, are you listening

Helen
yes I'm listening

Robyn
I am washing my hands because lately I have started
to pick at the fingers the little bit between the nail and
the finger, what is that part called, the bit by the nail
anyway there is blood and the taps are running and
all week I have been in and out and back and forward
and in the car – our car – and even the people at
reception know me and I have been there and the
phone rings the phone rings Helen and my mother is
in the room she has come to make sure I am okay,
and she has persuaded me home, the only hour hardly
I have been home since and I have just seen a dead

moth on the windowsill and picked it up and the
phone rings and the person says
and the person says

Beat.

Helen
what? what did they say?

Robyn
you don't know?

Helen
you're starting to freak me out

Robyn
they said something about you

Helen
what about me?

Robyn
they said something about you, four little words
they said
this is my mother she has taken the call
and the water from the sink is running over, it's
flowing over but no one is turning off the taps

Helen
what does she say?

Robyn
she says
she says she didn't make it
she says she didn't make it love.
she says

Beat.

Helen
what the fuck are you on about?
are you trying to piss me off?

Robyn
she says you didn't make it

Helen
so we are lost, we are in a bit of a pickle and you are
saying all this nonsense you are saying

Robyn
I'm standing by the window in our kitchen, in front of
the sink

Helen
stop it

Robyn
the water is overflowing

Helen
please just fucking stop it

Robyn
I see a dry moth on the windowsill, I pick it up

Helen
stop it

Robyn
I'm frightened

Helen
stop it

She thinks.

okay
okay okay
you are frightened, we had a trauma
of course you are frightened, it was horrible I'm
frightened
we nearly drowned but

Beat.

so there is this thing –
first of all, and I am no doctor but
I think you've got concussion
I actually do, when I said it before it was just but –
I think you might have concussion Robyn
now that's serious and I'm not saying it isn't but –
first you were sick
we both saw you vomit
that's a sign of concussion isn't it?

Robyn

you didn't make it

Helen

will you stop saying that?

Robyn

that's what she said
she took the call from the hospital, the senior doctor
you aren't here –
we aren't here –
I am in my kitchen I think or
maybe I am in our bed which has become my bed

Helen

no

Robyn

everything that was ours has become mine

Helen

please stop saying this

Robyn

you aren't here

Helen

what the hell do I do with that?
what the hell am I supposed to do with that?
you've got concussion.

Beat.

> listen
> there are lots of things that happen when you bang
> your head
> the boat rolled over
> it was a stupid boat
> I could see that you got hit as it turned, I could tell, I
> heard you cry out before –

Robyn
> I was concussed
> I was badly injured yes I think you are right
> I think I was the worst off, I think there is
> I think there is a moment where we are got out of the
> water, the coastal rescue did come, everyone came and
> everyone was worried about me, I could tell they were
> worried about me and you were there

Helen
> stop

Robyn
> I got better
> I was concussed and I got better
> and you didn't

Beat.

Helen
> what do you do when you are marooned on a tiny
> sand bank with your girlfriend and she starts to go
> crazy?
> that is a question for you angels. Tell me what to do?
> is there a handbook somewhere?
> she is convinced we have been here before but she
> survived.
> she survived, apparently I didn't
> anyone any suggestion for that?

Robyn
I hope I'm going crazy

Helen
no doubt about it.
utterly bonkers

Beat.

I'll get you some water
I am really not going to listen to much more of this.
Jesus

Robyn
I feel really thirsty

Helen
there's something not right with you, okay. I'll get you
help
I promise you I'll get you help
when the cloud clears, when I know how far we are
from the shore
I have a toffee in my pocket. Bit soggy but eat the
toffee
you need blood sugar, you've had a shock. Out there
in the water was a body shock. I should have given
you it ages ago.

Robyn
but I –

Helen
will you just eat the bloody sweet Robyn? just for
once don't argue

Robyn
I don't like toffees

Helen
do what you are bloody told

Beat.

She hands Robyn the toffee.

Robyn eats it.

It's a bit soggy and tastes of the sea. Helen looks at Robyn to make sure she's eating it.

Beat.

Helen
    my grandmother had this week where she utterly lost it
    maybe I never told you, I was a kid, eleven maybe
    did I tell you?

Robyn
    not sure

Helen
    she thought my grandfather was back, she was raving
    the staff in the home were devils
    it was frightening we were spirits or I don't know
    what we were, she screamed when she saw us
    honestly, she was hitting off the walls
    hallucinating and
    we thought that is it, she has gone, dementia or
    something
    we'll never get her back, that's what we thought
    my brother and I, she has gone
    mum and dad in this hourly conference
    turned out – few days later – it was a bladder
    infection
    it was a bloody bladder infection
    the infection in her blood
    course of antibiotics, and she came back, later, utterly
    came back to herself
    all I am saying is –

Robyn
    she went that mad?

Helen
she went bonkers, then some medicine and right as
rain

Robyn
is that true?

Helen
all I am saying

Robyn
can that happen?

Helen
all I am saying is something has happened with you
maybe you have an infection –

Robyn
I don't think –

Helen
maybe you hit your head
I think that's the most likely
maybe the water
do you have a headache?

Robyn
a bit

Helen
there we are then
concussion my bet, and whatever it is
we'll get it sorted

Robyn
it isn't a toffee it's a fruit pastel

Helen
even better

Robyn
it's a bit sweet

Helen
    I wish I had another. I'd shove it down your throat

Helen starts writing in the sand. She takes off her clothes and lays them out.

    rocks are easier than people, just in case you are
    wondering

Robyn
    I wasn't

Helen
    well they are

Robyn
    what are you doing?

Helen
    I am making an SOS sign that can be seen from the sky
    and don't shoot it down, don't tell me the million
    reasons why it won't work
    I need to do something

Beat.

Robyn
    we could try that woman again

Helen
    we could
    if we wanted
    we could try that woman again
    she is bonkers but go ahead

Robyn looks up.

Robyn
    no one will see it

Helen
    fuck's sake

Robyn
just saying, for them to see it they would have to be flying directly above

Helen
it is better to do something, isn't it? However futile. Another question for the angels, better to do something or not at all? Answer that. To die trying, or to die from not trying? Not that we are dying, it was a figure of speech. How to use your energy. I think we need to do something someone will realise we are missing soon, that's the thing, we have to remember the people who own the boat, this is just in case

Robyn
I don't feel concussed

Helen
oh but I am dead?

Beat.

Robyn
maybe you aren't dead

Helen
you think?

Beat.

Robyn
I hope not

Helen
well that is something, thanks for that

Robyn gets up and puts her arms around her.

Robyn
of course I hope not

Helen
I get fed up with this

Robyn
with this what?

Helen
with this imagination
all this
this dark stuff
you, there is always something to worry about
something you are chewing at
nothing is ever just –

Robyn
that isn't true

Helen tries to push her off.

don't be so angry

Helen
I'm not angry I'm just –
I'm really worried about you
I'm either worried or I'm really pissed off and I can't
work out which one it is
get off me

Robyn
please

Helen
try not to be so crazy.
it was a horrible accident okay, but it didn't happen

They hug each other.

Robyn kind of sobs.

it's okay
it's scary we have been through a trauma
it was horrible, when the boat went over it felt
impossible to survive for a moment or two but –
and sure nothing like this ever happened to us before

Robyn
it was just an accident. I know.

Helen
exactly
and we did make it.

She goes back to her SOS sign.

when the cloud clears someone should be able to see
this, I don't think they would have to be directly ahead
if they were in a plane over there or
maybe a birdwatcher with binoculars

Robyn
maybe

Beat.

how much can you remember?

Helen
of what?

Robyn
of the worst bit
of the bit when –

Helen
not much

Robyn
slipping from the boat, fighting for breath

Helen
somehow getting to the shore
feeling really buzzy then you vomiting

Robyn
under the water

Helen
nothing
just as I say it felt hard to survive for a second then

Robyn
you do remember something –

Helen
no
I don't
I don't

She comes back over to Robyn and they kiss.

I don't

Robyn
you must remember something, you said you were
sorry you didn't help me

Helen
okay I remember that bit but

Beat.

Robyn
you promise you don't –
because a second ago there

Helen
I promise I don't.

Beat.

Robyn
okay
okay I imagined it
the kitchen and the moth

Helen
you did imagine it

Robyn
the water pouring over the edge of the sink, the phone
call –

Helen
of course

Robyn
maybe this is the real and the other is the unreal
maybe as the boat went down and I could see you
were in trouble and I couldn't help you, maybe it was
then –
maybe it was then I imagined standing in the kitchen
and what it would be like if the worst happened and
my mother would come round – of course she would
and of course there would be trips back and forth to
the hospital and of course they would know me in
reception and maybe as I saw the moth, maybe it was
at that point that it got lodged in my brain
maybe the fucking utter terrible fear of what would
happen as I saw you going underwater and knowing I
couldn't help, maybe it was that fear that meant that I
kind of fast-forwarded on that trajectory, that I went
to the darkest place

Helen
you live your life in images
I always said you should write or paint or something

Robyn
I'm an academic

Helen
you live in books, you deal in stories

Robyn
okay maybe I took that image, and when I saw the
moth –

Helen
you live in the gothic novel that's why you are so
miserable

Robyn
yes okay but can the brain do that?

Helen
yours can

Robyn

really? Project a horrible image, give you a memory of
something that never happened?

Helen

do you remember when we looked at that house?
the one by the river
when you got your job

Robyn

vaguely

Helen

the one we put an offer in for, but didn't get

Robyn

it was a flat

Helen

it was on two floors

Robyn

it was tiny

Helen

we loved it, we would have loved it

Robyn

yes okay

Helen

remember the day, we went to the pub after, we
actually put the offer in from the pub and we sat with
a drink –
we imagined every little detail of our lives
we went over and over
how we would climb the stairs at the end of the day
how we would kick off our shoes as we went into the
bedroom
how we would watch the birds from the kitchen
window

449

how we would make love in the living room
how we would sit on the stairs with hot chocolate and
hot-water bottles listening to the rain
if we had a child
remember we thought then we might have a child –
we saw the child through the back
we could actually see –
I could imagine you working until late at night at the
little table in the front room, I could imagine having
to clear away our dinner things so you could work
there
I could imagine what that place would be like so full
to the brim with us

Robyn

yes

Helen

there are always parallel universes
every moment could split
I didn't die Robyn.
I got this surge of adrenaline
I was near to death but I got this incredible surge, this
superhuman surge, and I swam
I swam

Robyn

what *is* that patch on your finger called?
I want to chew on it again but I try not to. I want to
chew so much it is already bleeding
like I have taken it out on my finger
it's this patch beside the nail called and surely it's
called something or maybe it doesn't need a name,
maybe there is no reason for it to have a name except
that when you have picked and picked and torn with
your teeth for so many days when you go into the
pharmacist and say I would like some cream you can
say I would like some cream for this part, without

having to show her the place where you have almost
taken your own flesh off the bone
I am aware the woman is watching me
Helen is back on the shore, I have walked around I
suppose. I suppose I must have walked around –
I don't remember walking around but Helen says I
have concussion so everything is –
I look at the woman
she looks at me
I take a chair and sit down. There is a chair, I don't
see why I shouldn't sit down
there isn't a name for the part of your finger beside
your nail she says
there should be I say back and I am not surprised to
hear her voice. Her voice is exactly as I thought
maybe she says, maybe there should be a name but
there isn't
you aren't copying me now? I say
she looks at me she shrugs, she goes and gets a chair
she turns it the right way up
you bother me
you really bother me, I say to her
what do you want? she says
I want to know what you're doing here I say –
I want to know how you got here, and before you say
I live here, or I belong here or any of that –
you don't
you don't belong here. I know where I saw you, I
might have been temporarily, I might have for a
second forgotten where I'd seen you and I might be
pretending to Helen but –
it was the end of my garden
I saw you at the end of my garden
you turned up in a storm
don't look at me like that – she looks at me like
well she looks at me like she doesn't know what I'm

451

saying, which is rot because of course she knows she
knows every word
you came with a sleeping bag
you came with a bloody sleeping bag
you don't see as many women sleeping rough well you
worry don't you so of course I said of course, there is
a storm, please of course sleep in the garage, or where
you want
I have never seen you before she says
what we never met?
is everyone crazy? Is everyone crazy around here? Is
that the thing? I know I might have concussion but
there are some things I know. I know I saw you
she shrugs
it's important to say this to her
you turned up at the end of my garden
our garden, only
the garden that became mine
you turned up in the middle of a bad storm I saw you
before. I said to Helen I said to Helen there is a
person, a woman
I didn't say there is a woman I have seen before
I didn't say there is a woman who scares me a bit
no – bothers – me
there is a woman who came into my life after you
went
there is a woman who said I could make a wish

She stops.

can you actually look at me when we are talking?
my whole life is falling apart
I don't know what I am doing here or where I am
supposed to be but
if I am supposed to be here
I don't want to go crazy
is this a kind of taunting, a kind of ridiculing me with

is Helen alive or dead?
a kind of punishment for my grief?
I said I had seen you to the man I talk to
he isn't really a – well he is a kind of a counsellor
I'm not sleeping I see a counsellor
and this woman I told him, the first day I saw him
there was a storm and this woman with her sleeping
bag
she came and slept in the garage
she scared me because she said she would give me a
wish
and he said, the counsellor said, it sounds like
someone from a book
the old woman with the sleeping bag
it sounds like a character, an archetype
and he knows I write about books so I said yes okay
but this was real
and in the morning he said, when you went out to the
garage, was she there?
and when I said no
he said it was a dream
you saw a woman that scared you, it was like a kind
of shadow, your shadow, you saw what scared you in
yourself
like if I fell through the gaps and didn't get over this
if I didn't get over this like everyone thinks I should or
if I kind of fell to pieces and never found the way
back then maybe I would be wandering with my
sleeping bag
that is what he said
you're scared of being that woman, that is all.
she's a gremlin, a scary figure, someone to not become
but I said, in the dream if it was a dream, when the
woman came with her sleeping bag
she said she would give me a wish
I wanted that wish I wanted that wish so badly

453

more symbols from a story he said
I wish I had never told him about the books
I would reorganise the universe and to hell with the
consequences to have that wish, I said to him
I live here, she goes
on this island
but this place doesn't exist does it?
of course you live here
like you slept in my garden
three nights
second night I brought you some bread
so what I came to say, what I really came to say is
is this the wish? Because if this is the wish it's cruel,
it's a joke it's horrible.
I don't want it. I don't want this wish.
take it back.

I want to go home Helen
I don't trust anything here.
if this is concussion, I don't like it.
I don't believe it, that is the main problem
I don't believe the ground is actually here
that the sun is shining.
you didn't make it
that is all I can think of
I know it's awful to say and believe me it's been awful
but –
I know you didn't make it because these months have
been horrible and okay I hit my head and maybe you
will say I am the totally fucking insane one but –
we went out on that boat, you didn't want to, it was
my fault

Helen
shushh

Robyn
no

I couldn't remember it all at first, but little by little –
the condolence cards, the people smiling at me from
across the street, the hideous memorial, the nights I
couldn't sleep that I would have done anything

Helen
I've got help

Robyn
what?

Helen
there was a boat
just twenty minutes ago
I called you but
the clouds lifted just a bit and I could see
there was a boat out there
a little one, couple of people in it
I was like, here, we are marooned
they were so near I could shout
I was jumping up and down I was waving my arms

Robyn
you actually saw them?

Helen
they were so near

Robyn
there?

Helen
right there, you see. Someone is coming for us.
they will have seen that I was here and even if they
couldn't get to me, they'll get help.

Robyn looks out to the water.

Robyn
are you sure?

Helen
yes

Robyn
what did they look like?

Helen
it looked like two women

Robyn
two women like us?

Helen
no just two women
I suppose a bit like us, but no
two women in a boat, they are going to help us,
Robyn
will you please smile –?
you said we had to find a way off here and I think I
just did
I think we could be home by tomorrow

Robyn
tomorrow?

Helen
tonight, I mean tonight
we can get the dog and

Robyn
you said tomorrow –

Helen
well tonight or tomorrow

Robyn
are you okay?

Helen
I'm actually quite cold
I think the end of the adrenaline

I was jumping up and down, when I saw that boat
I think you were right, all that
I actually feel quite
we are looking after our neighbour's dog aren't we?

Robyn
come here
yes we are looking after a dog

Helen
and the dog is called Rosie?

Robyn takes off her cardigan and puts it around Helen.

Robyn
yes called Rosie
you should have had the toffee

Helen
and it barks all night

Robyn
she barks all night

Helen
will you just believe me then please? For once.
it doesn't always have to be you that knows
everything. I saw a boat and we are going to get some
help.

Beat.

Robyn
have you been sick?

Helen
no

Robyn
not at all?

Helen
not yet

Robyn
okay

Helen
my head is bleeding
I didn't notice it before but –

Robyn
oh god

Helen
I think I, did I hit the boat?

Robyn
your hair got tangled in the motor
christ Helen

Helen
my hair got tangled in the motor?

Robyn
that's what they said
but it was the internal damage to your liver that –

Beat.

Helen
I won't accept it

Robyn
neither you should

Helen
how can I accept it?

Robyn
of course you can't
how can you?
it's monstrous

Helen
impossible. Doesn't make sense

Robyn
  that's what I said

Helen
  it's utterly absurd, it's horrific it's, how could it have
  happened?
  we were out in a boat –
  we were just larking around
  it was an ordinary day

Robyn
  don't accept it
  I won't either

Helen
  you can't have a day that starts as ordinarily as ours

Robyn
  I've got concussion, you've got concussion

Helen
  it's not happening

Robyn
  we won't accept it

Helen
  and this, what is this?

Robyn
  I don't know about this
  I don't know about this

Beat.

Helen
  would you put your arms around me?

Robyn puts her arms around Helen.

  it can't be true anyway

Robyn
 it isn't then

Helen
 maybe we are both sick
 maybe we both got something in the water
 we have to remember my grandmother and her
 bladder infection

Robyn
 absolutely.

Beat.

 don't say anything else.

Helen
 we always said we would be truthful

Robyn
 okay

Helen
 I do remember something from under the water
 or after

Beat.

 I do have a sort of muscle memory
 pain, my hair getting tugged

Robyn
 my love

Beat.

Helen
 can it really . . . ?

Robyn
 shush.

Beat.

Helen
   it's so odd. I don't even feel like crying. I –

Beat.

   I've got a question

Robyn
   okay

Helen
   I heard you talking to the woman
   crazy lady
   I heard you

Robyn
   I don't know who she is

Helen
   what was the wish?
   if this is true then what was the wish?

Robyn
   what?

Helen
   you spoke to her about a wish, what was it?

Robyn
   not important

Helen
   tell me –

Robyn
   stupid

Helen
   we always said everything was honest between us
   what is the point if –

Robyn
   I can't

Helen
why can't you?
we both know that we have concussion, at least one
of us has concussion, we can't trust anything. What
was the wish?

Robyn
a day

Beat.

Helen
a day?

Robyn
yes

Helen
you wished for a day?

Robyn
yes

Helen
a single day?

Robyn
don't get cross with me

Helen
you could have asked for a year, a bloody lifetime,
you asked for a day?

Robyn
I don't know why

Helen
we have a day?

Robyn
I didn't think it would actually happen, how could it
happen

Helen
    a fucking day

Robyn
    don't get like that Helen it hasn't been easy

Helen
    a teensy-weensy tiny day?

Robyn
    I know it's

Helen
    why not ask for a minute, a microsecond

Robyn
    please stop

Helen
    why not waste it totally, you get a wish and you
    throw it away?

Robyn
    it wasn't a waste

Helen
    wasn't it?
    christ alive
    a day!
    this is what this is. Our day?

Robyn
    was there a boat?

Helen
    don't change the subject

Robyn
    I could still be concussed couldn't I?

Helen
    you aren't concussed –
    I might be but you

Robyn
your grandmother then –

Helen
we both know what is going on here
there's no avoiding it

Beat.

so what do we do, with this day?
this day you asked for
you asked for a day, and now you have it

Robyn
I don't want it

Helen
you don't want it?

Robyn
I didn't mean that I just meant –

Helen
is it a day in the middle of the accident, when it is
over will we be back in the water?

Robyn
how should I know?

Helen
and then I get to die again?

Robyn
please stop.

Helen
my hair being ripped in the fucking motor, is that
what happens?

Beat.

fucking hell
fucking fucking hell

Robyn
it's not enough, I know it's not enough

Helen
you're right, it's not enough

Robyn
it would never be enough
even if I had asked for eighty years it wouldn't be
enough

Helen
will I have to die again?

Robyn
don't ask me

Helen
I don't want to die again, if I already did it once

Robyn
I don't understand the rules

Helen
shit this is –

She starts to shake.

shit this is –

Robyn
please Helen

Helen
you shouldn't have done this
other people get over grief, why do you have to be the
one that can't stand it?

Robyn
I wasn't saying I couldn't stand it

Helen
everyone loses someone at some point don't they?

this isn't a unique experience, everyone goes through
the shit

Robyn

I know –

Helen

and I am not saying it wasn't bad but
why do you have to be the one that finds it
intolerable?
why do you have to be the one that does all this?

Robyn

I wasn't sleeping, I wasn't coping

Helen

for god's sake

Robyn

can't you find any sympathy?

Helen

I am the one that is fucking *dead*. Sorry if my
sympathy isn't completely focused around you.

Beat.

I'm just saying, it's quite extreme
it's quite an extreme thing to do
and I know it's been bad for you, but this, this isn't
exactly a picnic for me either
if I was – if I was what you said
then leave it
why not leave it?
why not fucking get over it?
why not leave me be?

Robyn

I'm sorry

Helen

jesus. You're sorry?

Beat.

She stands up.

> you were always extreme
> you say I talk too much but you –
> any experience you had was always worse
> you had a cold it was intolerable
> you had a pain it was beyond coping
> you had an exam it counted for twenty of mine –

Robyn
> that isn't true

Helen
> no wonder you couldn't do grief
> no wonder!

Robyn
> I fucking love you

Helen
> I fucking love you too.
> but this is, this –

Robyn
> what?

Helen
> this is fucked up

Robyn
> yes this is fucked up
> yes. Yes this is fucked up. Yes, do you think that you
> just dying wasn't fucked up?
> do you think that you just walking out of here,
> ceasing to exist, do you think that wasn't utterly and
> totally against the laws of how things should have
> been? And do you think I haven't asked a few times
> why the fuck could you, how could you have done
> that?

Helen

I'm not saying

Robyn

no you listen to me –
do you think I haven't asked, raged, Helen why the
fuck couldn't you swim?
you don't go out in a boat if you can't swim, you
don't fuck around over the side –
it wasn't an accident Helen you were mucking about

Helen

we both were

Robyn

I survived and you know what?
you left life in a total mess
there is no calm order that you left behind you totally
utterly crapped on me
no will, no bank details, where the fuck have you left
the key to your desk drawer you could start by telling
me that –

Helen

I can't remember

Robyn

of course you can't you couldn't organise yourself
when you were alive and yes maybe my experiences
were extreme, maybe I worried about things a bit
more but at least I got everything done
I have a will
I know my bank details. I have a file, if I had died,
you would be able –
I didn't even have your mother's number, not that
these things

Helen

it's on the wall

Robyn

in the hospital, do you think you should call her
parents yes probably where the fuck is their number

Helen

on the wall

Robyn

it should have been on the wall, it wasn't on the wall
of course it should have been on the wall, that is
where we keep all the numbers
it's not on the wall because it is to do with *you*, it is to
do with *you* and therefore it isn't easy, it isn't possible
for anyone else because all you ever thought about
was yourself and hence you died
you died because you didn't fight hard enough
you didn't fight through it Helen and I will never
forgive you –
you should have fucking fought, and swum and got
your head out of that motor and told your liver not to
pack in and bloody lived
you should have bloody lived.

Beat.

sorry but that is what I think

Pause.

Helen

fucking hell, so it's my fault?

Robyn

fuck it yes.

Beat.

Helen

I hate you sometimes

Robyn

I hate you too.
the day you died, I was so angry.

Beat.

and don't think it's just me. We're all pissed off with
you. Your mother
your brother is on antidepressants
your dad has hardly been out
but it's me, actually if you want to know
the one they are all worried about
I think I am fine but they think not
a woman comes to the garage at the bottom of the
garden
our garden, the garden that has become mine, that has
become only mine
our garden but it is mine now in a way I don't want
anyway a woman has come with her pathetic- looking
sleeping bag and it is really bloody raining
and I know it is bad, and she is probably homeless,
and I am worried about her, which I realise is a new
thought, a thought that for once isn't about my
fucking pain, yes Helen died but I can think about
another person and I shouldn't do it but I say yes you
could sleep in the garage, only the fucking garage of
course I should have done it, yes you can sleep there –
and the next day I take her out bread and some tea
and she says would you like a wish
and I fucking say yes Helen and okay I fuck it up
because you know what I never thought it would
happen
it can't happen
you can't get a day back
it's as impossible as you going in the first place
there is a strange place called grief and all the rules
are changed.

so I made a wish
I fucking made a wish

Beat.

Helen
I don't like to hear of you not coping

Robyn
well get used to it

Helen
how bad is it?

Robyn
bad
lining up pills bad
not getting out of bed bad it's

Helen
still looking after the dog?

Robyn
not really

Helen
tell me you didn't have her put down –

Robyn
of course I didn't, I took her to a friend's

Helen
because she's not ours

Robyn
I know she's not ours
she's with Toby

Helen
who's that?

Robyn
he lives further along the road, please don't forget
everything

Helen

she'll come back fat

Robyn

she isn't coming back, she isn't our dog anyway
the last thing I wanted was a dog to die on me, ours or
not ours, and I forget all about her and to be honest I
think she blames me
she looks at me like, what on earth is wrong with
you?

Beat.

you don't know what it is –
extreme widowhood, you have no idea

Beat.

I didn't mean
I realise of course
but nothing ever happened to us as big as this

Helen

what now, if I tell you I am scared? Alright for you,
you got your wish but –

Robyn

I don't know
don't be, please don't be scared.
I guess whatever it is, has already happened.

Beat.

Helen

I won't be scared
but I am glad you at least realise that being scared is a
possibility –
that being scared might in fact be normal, that it
might not all be about you

Robyn

I don't want you to be scared

Helen
I don't want to be scared either, truth be told

Beat.

I'll try to remember where the key to my drawer is

Robyn
thank you

Beat.

you know I didn't mean it

Beat.

Helen
yes I know that.
but I didn't mean it either –
I certainly didn't mean it
it's fucking shit.

Robyn
you could say that.

Beat.

Helen
where do you think you are?

Robyn
I don't know
in the house
I would say I am asleep but I don't sleep
I haven't been asleep even for a second I don't think
for months –
I don't know where I am
I could be in the garden
I could be in the garage, she could have tied me up or
I could be in bed
I suppose I am probably in the kitchen
maybe I am by the sink

473

Helen
    where am I?

Robyn
    I don't know that either

Helen
    where am I Robyn?

Beat.

Robyn
    you're in a grave
    your mother wanted a grave
    I said I thought you wouldn't mind, do you mind?

Helen
    where is it?

Robyn
    in her village
    I don't go there much, I should go there more, to be
    honest I find your mother –
    she asks what the hell we were doing out in a boat
    and I find I don't have an answer.
    we were mucking about I suppose
    we were treating life far too trivially and we got
    caught
    we didn't realise that you shouldn't do anything
    that you should stay inside that you should hang on
    to each other
    that's what we should have done
    stayed under our duvet not left our bedroom
    never gone out –

Helen
    my brother would never take antidepressants

Robyn
    well he does now
    he really does

Beat.

Helen

I'm not sure what I am supposed to do with all this –
I don't actually know
I don't actually, I mean what . . .?

Robyn

I don't know either

Helen

you don't get taught do you, you don't get prepared
this isn't exactly
I mean, one of those situations –

Beat.

how much more of our day do you think we have
got?

Robyn

a few hours?

Helen

oh hell.

Robyn

and that's when you think about *when*
and you realise how much worse it is to know that
you are going to lose someone, that all those people
that stay nights beside a bed or watch someone die
from cancer, that their lot is worse because if it is
unthinkable to lose the person you love, it is even
worse to know that it is going to happen.
and I know I don't get a second wish, of course you
don't get a second wish. Who in the world of
children's stories hundreds and hundreds of stories
about wishes, whoever heard of someone who can get
a second wish just because they didn't like how the
first one turned out? But anyway I go and I find her
and I ask –

I find the woman, she is standing with her sleeping
bag just like I first saw her in my garage
woman, I say, I don't care who you are or if you are a
projection or my fear or a person in a story I haven't
written yet but –
this is a nightmare, you brought me to a nightmare
this isn't a wish
if I am to be here and I am to be here with Helen then
take away the muscle memory please kind spirit or
angel or please let me forget. Let me forget what is to
come later.
let me be with Helen
let me be innocently with Helen on a beach.
take away everything I know if you need to,
everything I ever learnt
because all I can smell is dying flowers, even when I
move them, all the whole world smells of dying
flowers and this cardigan this widow's cardigan the
only thing I can ever put on in the morning –
if this is to be with Helen then let it be a free day
free of all of that.
please whoever you are
if I have a wish, that is what I wish.

Nothing happens.

Robyn looks about.

wish lady?

Helen has gone.

Helen?
Helen?

Robyn looks about her.

She looks panicked.

no don't take her away –
I didn't mean

the counsellor said you were a figment of my, that I
should argue with you, if he got that wrong or
okay I wasn't supposed to argue but I didn't mean –
Helen?
Helen?
fucking hell Helen come back?

Helen?
I'll do anything, I'll tear up the universe, I'll start
again
HELEN
I didn't mean it, I didn't mean to say I didn't want my
wish, I just meant, to use the day you would have to
not know, to be ignorant wouldn't you –?
I get it, you don't argue with wishes
I get it, you don't argue with the universe –
there is no argument
let me finish the day

She looks around.

Still nothing.

She looks around again.

More nothing.

please?
please –
so where am I, if she isn't here?
I'm in my bed –
I'm standing at my window –
I'm in the kitchen –
water is overflowing from the sink
why am I still here in this place?
alright I accept
is that what you want to hear?
I accept
she died

she died, she died hideously, and alone later in hospital
she died incrementally over days –
she got her hair caught in the motor and then mashed
up her insides she
she fucking died, I wasn't there she fucking died
I accept
I accept
bring Helen back please
she fucking died
she is dead for ever and ever
I FUCKING ACCEPT
she is dead for ever and ever and ever and ever and
ever
and I . . .

Helen comes back on. She is carrying some sticks.

Helen

the light is nearly fading, I thought we could make a
fire.
I found this old set, looks like it was a barbecue or
something

Robyn

oh god

Helen

what?

Robyn

nothing
I thought you'd gone that's all

Helen

I have.
we know I have
we might as well finish our sentences

Beat.

but there are a few hours left

Robyn
a few hours, is that all?

Helen
a few hours is a few hours
it's a small thing but it is a thing
sit by the fire with me
if I can do this, you can

Robyn
oh god

Helen
shush. Nothing okay, we say nothing.

Robyn
alright but
alright but

Helen
alright.

Beat.

They say nothing.

Robyn
how are you going to light it?

Helen
what?

Robyn
the fire. Two women lighting a fire
when have we ever been able to do something like
that?

Helen
ah ah, my discovery
we can't, we are rubbish at things like that
but we aren't *we* today.
I mean this isn't –
this is a place where the rules are fucked

479

a liminal place, a shimmer
I like toffees, you like fruit pastilles actually I would
never have had a fruit pastille or a toffee in my pocket
when did I ever have a sweet in my pocket?
there wasn't an island here –
there wasn't an island there, if there was an island
here we would've been okay
so I think we can probably light a fire
maybe with our fingertips or
look
matches
I have matches in my pocket of course I do
we could probably find a steak dinner if we looked
hard enough in the sand
you want water –
there is water

Robyn
we couldn't do this before

Helen
we didn't realise where we were before
we thought it was real

Robyn
and don't tell me there'll be a day when I will feel
better and waking up and you not being there will
even feel normal, and perhaps one day the sun will be
out and I will hear birds again and fuck it I have read
the books, I know that one day this –

Helen
shush

Robyn
is that why you are here? is that why this –
to tell me that there are better things ahead, that I
won't always feel like this and if so don't, don't say
anything unless you have got a big mechanical arm

that can reach up to the sun and roll it the other way
around the world
turn the clocks back

Helen
I've got nothing
I've got nothing Robs
I won't say any of that

Robyn
will it get better?

Helen
I don't know

Robyn
it's monstrous, every day
I have to crawl through the hours

Helen
it *is* monstrous
it shouldn't have happened

Robyn
it's a monstrous world, and it's not enough

Beat.

Helen
take the matches and light the fire
it's getting dark

Robyn
is that it?

Helen
yep
pretty much
the day will soon be over.